Creating an Heirloom

Writing Your Family's Cookbook

BY

Wendy A. Boughner Whipple

PublishAmerica
Baltimore

First printing

ISBN: 1-4137-4894-5
PUBLISHED BY PUBLISHAMERICA, LLLP
www.publishamerica.com
Baltimore

Printed in the United States of America

This book is lovingly dedicated to the ones who inspire nearly everything I do, my family and friends; to my daughter Diana, who has taught me to look at the world in different ways; to my husband, Marc, whose unshakable faith that I could do this held me up; to Mom and Dad, who are always there whenever I need them; and to Magda, who gave me something utterly beyond measure. Without *all* of your love and encouragement, none of this would have happened. Thank you.

Acknowledgments

I would like to extend my thanks to the following: Rachel Scoville from Athena Publishing, for her help in answering questions about how small publishers work with families to put their cookbooks together; Karen Velthuys and Lory Trost from Gateway Publishing and G&R Publishing, respectively, for taking the time to answer questions about how the larger publishers work with families; everyone at PublishAmerica for the opportunity to publish this book; Ali Visona, for her patient genius with the camera; the Matteson Public Library for their assistance in ordering everything I needed to research this book; and Joe Loucka of OL Communications, Inc., the best ISP guy around. And last, but never least, to my critics, proofreaders, cheerleaders, friends, and others who have provided me with inspiration over the years: Mom, Dad, Marc, Julie, Marilyn, Norma, Arlene, Judy, Lady Isadora, Matt, Magda, Liz, Ricky, and so many others…you are all the best, and I am grateful for everything.

Table of Contents

Introduction

This book is based and greatly expanded upon the web page I wrote, which has been online since May 2001. I have had many people contact me to tell me how much it has helped them when they made their own cookbooks, and I loved hearing from all of them. It is my hope that people will find this even more helpful, and also easier to reference while in the middle of a project, so they won't have to go back and forth to the web page.

Whether you realize it or not, you're about to create a priceless heirloom. Maybe you won't see it that way when you're done, but the next generation, and certainly the generation after that, will. You are preserving something very, very precious. Just remember to have a little fun while you're doing it!

If you can use a word processor, you can create a very professional-looking cookbook. If computing isn't your best skill, there are options in this book for you, too. Taking things step by step will make it easy.

Writing a cookbook for your family is both as easy as it sounds and fairly tricky to achieve. There are all sorts of things that will go wrong, unexpected things you hadn't counted on, and uncooperative people to handle. But *you can do it.* And I can help.

Wendy A. Boughner Whipple
http://www.CreatingAnHeirloom.com

Chapter One
Which Cookbook Will You Write?

So you've decided to sit down and gather your family's treasured recipes. Good for you! The aromas from the kitchen can evoke more memories than mere words can. Talking to family about some of their favorite dishes and recollections will provide you with a rich tapestry that you can craft into a cookbook. Your cookbook, an heirloom in the making, will be something everyone in your family will appreciate. Later generations will praise you for your efforts and your foresight in collecting it all in the first place.

The question then becomes, where do you start? You need a clear goal in mind, or your project will be an enormous mish-mash of intentions and ideas. Are you collecting recipes from a certain part of your family—just your mom's side, just your dad's, your side of the family, your side and your spouse's? Once you have that decided, you can think about theme. Really, you don't need one, but it can help you stay on track. If you're intending for the book to be done for a Christmas gift, you could choose that holiday as your theme. In that Christmas cookbook could be included various special-occasion recipes and the sweet treats that are only made once a year. If you're intending a family reunion cookbook, your focus could be on the more historical aspects of the recipes and the people who made them. Perhaps you want to make a single cookbook to welcome a new bride into your family and want the family favorites from both families. All of those ideas lend themselves to a theme in both recipe content and look of the cookbook.

Keep in mind that you need to plan in advance for these occasions. If your sibling gets engaged, consider asking folks to contribute recipes as soon as possible, so that you will have plenty of time to get the book finished before the wedding. And don't start a Christmas gift in November! Three months is the *absolute minimum* time you should allow yourself to put your cookbook together; six months is a much more reasonable time frame.

What kind of cookbook will you write? Consider these occasions:

Holidays

If you and your family love holidays, then why not build a family cookbook around your favorite holiday? From Mardi Gras to Mother's Day, Kwanzaa to Candlemas, Hanukkah to Halloween, there's a calendar full of reasons to celebrate your family and the food they cook. If you can't decide on a single holiday, set your cookbook up as a "calendar" with each chapter being a certain holiday and the foods you serve for it. A holiday cookbook could be specifically special occasion recipes, or just an excuse to create a cookbook. That also helps coordinate your clipart, and there's a lot of holiday-oriented art available.

Seasons, similar to holidays, may have foods that are particular to that season, like your mom's fruit salad she makes in the summertime, or the pheasant Uncle Rick makes every fall. Your cookbook could follow the seasons, or focus on a single season for its recipes.

Bridal Showers

For one of my bridal showers, the hostess asked each guest to bring a recipe (at least one), so that the new bride (me) would have a ready-made collection of tried-and-true recipes. This was a very special gift, one I treasure. If you take that same idea and put the recipes into a small photo album, leaving room for pictures from the shower, and present that to the bride, it will be even more special for her. You could choose to decorate this book with the bride-to-be's favorite color, or, if you know them, the colors chosen for the wedding. This would also make a lovely scrapbook cookbook. There are lots of wedding-themed scrapbook supplies. You are bound only by your imagination and time.

Weddings & Anniversaries

As a wedding gift to the new couple, you could be more elaborate, especially if you have a few months before the wedding is to take place. Gather recipes from the entire guest list, if you can. Then, they will not only have a wonderful and thoughtful gift, but also a useful record of who helped celebrate their special day. Use their wedding colors for the book.

You could present the same idea at an anniversary party, whether it's the 5th, 25th, or 50th. Any time is a good time to tell people you care about them. Anniversary "milestones" have traditional gifts. You can use them as a theme in your art or colors. Some of the traditional gifts for those milestones are:

First anniversary—paper
Fifth—wood
Tenth—tin or aluminum
Fifteenth—crystal
Twentieth—china
Twenty-fifth—silver
Fiftieth—gold
Sixtieth and seventy-fifth—diamonds.

Baby Showers

Basically, take the same idea for the bridal shower, and use it for the baby shower. Just ask your guests to contribute kid-friendly recipes, or recipes for meals that can be prepared quickly and easily (since the new parents won't have time for elaborate meals).

Graduations

This is a wonderful occasion to commemorate: a rite of passage, as children leave home to start their own lives. And if you give them your recipes ahead of time, you will save them a fortune on long-distance charges. (I was constantly calling Mom for recipes once I was out of college. It gets expensive!)

This is an easy theme to plan for. You know when the person is likely to graduate, so plan for it accordingly. If you make several, you will also have ready graduation gifts for other family members who will be graduating in the future.

Family Reunions

This is perhaps the most common reason to compile a family cookbook. Since reunions are frequently planned well in advance, you should also have plenty of time to put your masterpiece together. Reunions are also a great time to take photos of all those relatives, perhaps for use in the next cookbook. It's also a good time to have older family members identify people in old photos.

You can gather recipes and stories at reunions, too. If you've just bought this, and you have a family reunion coming up, be sure you take a notebook with your camera, and write down some of those stories. Then you'll have them when you write your cookbook. (Don't forget to write down the date, and who told the story.)

Lots of people use the selling of cookbooks to pay for the cost of the reunion itself. The cookbook/fundraiser publishers can help you with that. *See* **Chapter Eleven, Publishing Resources**.

Beyond the simple idea of family reunion, there is also the historical theme. You could dig deeper than the recipes themselves and learn more about the lives of the people who cooked and ate them. The cookbook could be a family history, a genealogical record, sprinkled with recipes and memories. If you haven't started researching your family tree, this could be an excellent excuse to get started. (As there are a number of truly fine genealogy how-to books, I won't get into collecting that information here.)

Other Themes

If you are from an old Southern (New England, Midwestern, etc.) family, you could build a cookbook around that theme, and request dishes that are traditional for your part of the world. Use regional clipart, or symbols that are synonymous with that region or state, like the magnolia in Mississippi or lobster in Maine. You could pull regional history into your cookbook as well, instead of more general historical references, to paint a more complete picture of your family and the places and times in which they lived.

Perhaps you have a family name like Appleby, Baker or Rivers. A playfully themed cookbook could be centered on your surname and be reflected in the art you choose. Many surnames have occupational meanings, for instance, coopers made barrels, fletchers made arrows, and chandlers made candles. What do you have in your surname that lends itself to a theme?

If your family has a specific ethnic heritage (or heritages), you could choose to concentrate on that, as well. Future generations may find that ethnic heritage diluted by increasing assimilation into American melting-pot multi-culture. Wouldn't it be a shame for the generations yet to be to miss out on some of those truly marvelous ethnic dishes?

> TIP: If you are going to create a themed cookbook, look for clipart (check out the Dover clipart books) that helps accent that theme. Whether your theme is a holiday, wedding or region, you can find art that will match it.

Small Families

It is entirely possible that you don't have any old family recipes, or that the family members that you could have asked for recipes have passed away. Or maybe your family is just small, or really spread out, or simply not close knit. If you still want to make a family cookbook, don't let those things stop you! Take the dishes your family loves and include those. Write about the birthday cake that your child asks for every year, or the special barbecue you make for Independence Day, and what your family does that day. What do you serve for Christmas dinner? Was there a special celebration for some family milestone?

Your cookbook could be something that you put together out of love for a child leaving home. It could be a tribute not necessarily to your entire family tree, but to your immediate family. The cookbook you write could be a legacy for grandchildren and great-grandchildren you haven't even met yet. You don't need an army of relatives to make a family cookbook, just a lot of love...and patience.

You are limited only by your imagination. Hopefully you are now filled with inspiration, and ready to begin!

Chapter Two
Getting Started

You're committed to the cookbook, excited about the project, and can't wait to get started. Hold on; there are a few things that need to be done first. Before you contact anyone, decide on what your deadline is, and make sure you're allowing at *least* three months' time. Four to six months is more realistic. Three months allows for a month to gather recipes, a month to enter them, at least two weeks to proofread, and another two weeks to publish—and that assumes everything runs smoothly and there's no wait at the printer or problems with your own binding equipment. The longer your book, the longer the process will take. If you know it will take longer to gather, type, and proofread, plan accordingly!

Then, consider this: How big do you want the cookbook to be? Are there enough family members interested in this project to share their recipes? If so, you're all set. If not, you will probably need to persuade some folks, and visit others. If you have an enormous family, getting everyone to contribute a single recipe will make for a sizable cookbook. If your family is not so abundant, are there enough people to contribute a few recipes? There were 19 living contributors to the cookbook I wrote for my family, and 260 recipes, filling 96 pages (48 double-sided pages). That calculates to not quite 14 recipes per person. Some folks only sent me one or two recipes; others were really generous and sent more. If you don't have an amount in mind, now's the time to think about that.

You will next need to make a list of family members you want to contact. A good place to start is with your Christmas card list, if you have one, or your address book. Decide if you want your cookbook to include just one branch of the family or the whole tree. But consider this: if you choose to keep it narrow in scope, there is a strong possibility that someone's feelings could be hurt for being excluded. If your goal is to be totally inclusive, share your list with someone who can suggest anyone you may have forgotten.

If you are planning to build your cookbook around a theme, be sure you put that in your letter to family members requesting recipes. With a holiday cookbook, for instance, you may want to ask for special occasion recipes, and things that folks only make for that holiday.

Then, draft your letter of request. Phone calls are certainly more personal, but if your family is far-flung, it will also be expensive. Too, if you write a letter, you won't forget to tell the person something. Include in your letter your goal and your motivations, and explain what you are looking for. Name your deadline, and the date you state should be a *month sooner* than you actually need to have everything in hand, giving procrastinators a chance to send things to you. Include a self-addressed stamped envelope; you increase your chances of getting something back that way. If you're concerned about the length of the cookbook, ask for a specific number of recipes. Asking for between 2 and 5 recipes isn't a hardship; asking for 10 might be pushing it; asking for 20 is a little outrageous.

> TIP: Here's a mistake of mine to learn from: I gave everyone a deadline of November for a book I wanted to publish in December. *Do not* give yourself so little time that you end up rushed. Allow at least three months: that way you can give everyone more time to help you, and you have more time to put it together. Tell people you want the recipes a month sooner than you need them. This will give stragglers a chance to get things to you. If you want to have everything in hand by November, give them a deadline of October, and stick to it!

There were children who were at home or away at college and didn't cook. I asked them for the recipes that they wanted included, then went to the family member who had it and said I had a special

18

request for a certain recipe. Don't forget to ask your young family members about the things *they* love the most. Some kids may even have recipes of their very own!

Don't be too disappointed if people express enthusiasm for what you're trying to do, and then never quite get around to sending you the recipes they promised. And don't take it personally! Three years after my initial request, after much begging and many threats, my older brother has finally given me the recipes I asked for, but our mother had to fly to San Diego to get them. The following is a sample letter, based on the one I wrote to my family; please feel free to alter it to suit your purposes.

Dear (Grandma/Aunt/Brother/Cousin),

Family history is sort of what's prompting this letter. I am trying to put together a family cookbook. The goal is to have it assembled for Christmas, so I can give them as gifts. What I would really appreciate from you is recipes. ANY recipes, not just special occasion ones. Anything you remember someone making that you loved, things that you love to make yourself, that sort of thing. If it's a recipe you got from someone else, please tell me who that family member is. I'm trying to make this personal—"Aunt Shirley's Noodles," for instance.

Also, if you have any stories you want to share about special recipes, dinners you can remember as being extra special, cooking triumphs or disasters...anything like that.

This is a special and important project for me, and I hope you will contribute to it. You'll get a copy, of course! If at all possible, I'd like to have the recipes by the end of November, so I can get it all put together by Christmas. You can write them out, photocopy them, e-mail them or whatever's easiest; I don't want this to be a burden on the people I am asking to assist me. You have my address, but in case it's not handy: (my address, and email address).

I really appreciate anything you can send me. Thanks in advance!

Love,

Another reason for making adequate time for this is because the unexpected will happen. Life has a way of interfering when we're working on other things. By giving yourself a large enough time frame, you also allow for additions to the list of people you're including. (Your second cousin just heard about your project from Aunt Ruth and is going to send you recipes next week.)

Organization

Being organized will help you a great deal. Set up a workspace for yourself, and keep it tidy. If you work best at the kitchen table, be sure that you can move everything easily when it's suppertime. Keep all your materials together. Any notes you have should also be easily accessible. An accordion file works perfectly for this.

Your list of contacts should include name, phone number and/or email address, and address. This list will enable you to check and see who has or hasn't sent in recipes. Those that haven't responded at all should be contacted by phone or by email, to see if they intend to send anything at all. Ideally, everyone you contact will want to participate.

The bottom line is that if you keep everything organized (so that looking for something doesn't become a scavenger hunt all over the house) your project will flow much more smoothly. There are things I did the first time that I really wish I had done differently. Being more organized is one of them.

Checklist:

Have you:

1. Decided on your deadline, and given yourself adequate time to work on the project?

2. Made a list of family members you want to contact, either personally or through correspondence?

3. Do you have a theme? If it requires specific recipes, be sure to say so!

4. Drafted your letter of request?

5. Mailed the letter with a self-addressed stamped envelope (SASE) enclosed?

6. Set up a workspace?

7. Gotten an accordion file (or something similar) to keep all your recipes and papers together?

Chapter Three
Other Sources

There are plenty of other places to look for additions to your cookbook beyond what the people you have contacted think to send. When I went through my mother's recipes, I ended up including a few that she hadn't volunteered, because those recipes were things I remembered and were special to me. Think about the recipes that are special to you, ask others to do the same, and make sure they're included in your cookbook.

If you have access to family members' recipe boxes, ask to borrow them for a day or so, and thumb through them. You might find a gold mine in that rusty tin box, kitchen drawer, or old shoebox, but you won't find anything if you don't look.

> TIP: Be sure to take a notebook if you go see those family members; you never know what stories might come out of the visit! Notebooks and cameras are two things family historians should never be without.

Borrowing someone's recipe collection takes tact and understanding. Don't expect everyone to happily hand over a lifetime of recipes just because you want to borrow them. Explain what you are doing, why you want them, and assure them that no harm will come to the recipes. If you are going to scan all of the contents, *be sure you put them back in then box in the order that you found them.* Offer to give the person a copy of the CD you archive them on, even if they don't have a computer. If it is your goal to archive the recipes to CD, tell the owner that you think the contents are worth saving and protecting forever; that might go a long way to convince them that you will take care of the collection.

If your family member just can't bear to let a collection (it is likely very precious to them, too) leave their hands, sit down with them if you can and go through its contents one by one. Here's your chance to ask lots of questions and take lots of notes. Write down some of the recipes; record the stories. She (or he) may come across a card from an old friend, and a girlhood story may come of it. She may find a card from her grandmother or mother-in-law, and give you insight on that person, things you never would have known if not for that visit. Take your camera and take pictures of your relative with the recipe collection. Recipes themselves don't photograph well, you really need a scanner for that. If you have a laptop (or one you can use) and a scanner (likewise), take them with you and scan everything while you're there.

Recipe Boxes

If you get a chance to look through someone's recipe box, here are some things to look for: Recipes marked "Aunt Jane's _____" (ask who Aunt Jane is/was, and get a surname) or "Grandma Smith's ___," stained recipe cards—the ones that have been well used, or recipes that were written with a fountain pen, those are almost certainly old. If you're not sure what that looks like, check for faded ink and writing in graceful script. Penmanship was something people used to take pride in!

If you do find recipes with names on them, be sure to ask the owner who that person was. Even if it was a friend of the family, the memories that come out of it will be very special. Maybe "Thelma" baby-sat your dad when your uncle was born, or "Jean" was the Brownie Scout leader when your mom was in the Brownies.

Take note, too, of what the recipes are written on. There are sometimes clues about the age of the item on it. Recipes written on the backs of bank deposit slips will sometimes have the date. If you find newspaper clippings, look carefully to find some indication of what newspaper and when it's from. If you do find this information, *document it!*

On a trip to my aunt's a few years ago, I noticed that she had the recipe box that had belonged to her mother (my dad's mom). I asked if I could borrow it, swearing to take good care of it and return it as soon as humanly possible. Mind you, this wasn't a jog down the street; my aunt lives in Mississippi and I live in Illinois. She reluctantly (I would have been, too!) allowed me to take it home so I could scan the contents. I spent several days scanning them as soon as I got home so I could get her box back to her. I also made a CD with all the recipes on it and sent a copy with the box. Because I was in a hurry to return the box, I forgot to photograph the box itself. (Don't make my mistake; take several pictures to be certain at least one turns out. I ended up purchasing a box of the same style and used the box as the illustration for the CD's jewel box.) When I sent it back to my aunt, I wrapped the box in bubble wrap, crumpled newspaper around it, and insured the contents for $100. I had it for less than a week, and Aunt Janice was pleased to get a CD of the archived recipes along with the return of the treasured box. I also gave copies of the CD to my dad's other sister and my mom.

In that recipe box were recipes from my grandmother's mother-in-law, her aunt, and her sister, as well as from friends Grandma had made when she and Grandpa lived in Illinois, where my dad and his sisters grew up. I have a record of her handwriting, too, which makes the contents of that recipe box as precious to me as to her daughter.

Recipe Binders or Notebooks

Many cooks also have small binders that were made for keeping recipes in. These notebooks often come with envelopes for storing recipes clipped from the newspaper or magazines. Other cooks may simply use a notebook of the sort used for school. I have also seen recipes written in ledger books.

Newspaper clippings can be especially interesting finds if they include the date somewhere on it, or the name of the newspaper. Clippings should definitely be scanned before they deteriorate worse. Handle them with care; newsprint becomes fragile with age.

NOTE: From an archivist's perspective, newspaper should be removed from contact with other papers. Acid migration (the

> shifting of acid in the newspaper to other papers near it) will eventually destroy the other things it touches. You can see evidence of acid migration in the brown stains newspaper leaves on other papers.

If you are fortunate enough to have an ancestor's handwritten cookbook, a book that she has already written her treasured recipes in, look at it very closely. Likely as not, there will be more in that collection than just recipes. Some of those books were also diaries of sorts and may contain some of the simplest of historical facts, like a complaint about the price of meat. She may have even kept her household accounts in it. There is a huge historical treasure there. It could even become a research project and a book on its own, including bits of that woman and her family's history, where they lived and how. The more history you can add to that (family, local, national and world), the richer it will all be.

If the recipes are really outdated (and they probably will be), perhaps they could be included in your family cookbook with a bit of modernizing. Be sure to include both the original version and your updated one. Instead of "cook in a hot oven till done," your instructions might read "bake at 400°F for 25 minutes, or until golden." Please note that experimentation will be necessary here, so you know if your updated version actually works. Be sure to ask older family members who knew that cook if they remember any of the dishes in her handwritten cookbook. And don't forget to archive that original!

Handwritten Recipes in Books

There are unexpected sources of recipes in books. People often mark the pages of a favored cookbook with slips of paper with recipes written on them. When my grandmother died, I received some of her cookbooks. I was flipping through her copy of *The Joy of Cooking* and found three handwritten recipes, and one more in Meta Givens' *Modern Encyclopedia of Cooking, Volume 2*. Unfortunately, two of the four recipes are so cryptic as to be unusable without some research, one of those merely being a list of ingredients with no instructions.

If you find such a recipe, all is not lost. You might be able to find a similar recipe in another source. If you can puzzle out what the recipe might be for, you should be able to find something in a large cookbook that will help. It turns out that one of the recipes I found is for homemade crackers.

Notations Written in Cookbooks

Often, old cookbooks will have notations next to recipes that were used often, like substitutions of ingredients, or comments like "Very good!" or "No." I have seen notations indicating when that recipe was served, like at Christmas or Thanksgiving. So look in those old cookbooks: who knows what you might find?

Oral Tradition

It is entirely possible that some of the older cooks will have especially treasured recipes memorized, or not written down anywhere at all. Thanksgiving and Christmas are perfect times to spend a day in the kitchen with your family, writing down what they do, how much they use (you may have to interrupt them, and measure that quantity of flour in their hand!), what the temperature on the stove or in the oven is. They may have learned how to make that item from their mother or grandmother. If you don't record it, it might be lost forever.

Secret Family Recipes

What do you do with a family member that has a secret recipe and doesn't want to share? First, try explaining that you are trying to preserve a special part of your family's history for future generations. Help them understand that you believe the "secret recipe" should be preserved for future generations. Don't say, "I want to save the recipe so that if you die tomorrow, the family still has it."

If, even after you have carefully explained your motivations, and genuine desire to preserve something of your family's heritage forever, they still don't want to share, don't push. All that will do is make you both unhappy. Let it be. They might change their minds on their own, especially when they see what a fabulous job you have done on the finished cookbook. They may approach you about doing a second edition, one that includes all their secret recipes....

Archiving

I cannot stress strongly enough the importance of scanning the contents of old recipe boxes or files. It may not seem like a big deal now, but it just might later. In the case of my grandmother, there were two daughters and a daughter-in-law who would have liked to have the box. The older daughter is the one who has it, but since I was able to scan the cards, my mom and the younger aunt now have electronic copies of the same recipes.

If you do find notations in cookbooks, scan those as well, and record somewhere (like in a text file on the CD with the scanned page) what book it came from and who the book had belonged to. If the book is not one in your possession, also include who the present owner of the book is. Again, this may not seem important at the time, but if something were to happen to the book, you have the handwritten notes archived on CD, as well as references to what notes are in which book, if you need to find them later.

Because I tend to be very cautious, I have copies of some of my irreplaceable documents and photos scanned, with extra CDs made and kept away from home. If we had a disaster here, without those redundant copies, we'd lose everything.

Archiving and digital restoration are time-consuming and sometimes frustrating tasks when the cards don't scan well due to the age and wear on the card. It's worth it to do your best. Interested family members will be thrilled. And if you are not lucky enough to have a scanner of your own, it's a fairly safe bet that someone in your family does, and would be willing to scan everything for you. Whenever you enlist the aid of someone for anything, be sure that they are aware of what exactly it is you want them to do. Have them read the relevant chapter(s) of this book, if you're afraid you're not being clear. *Please see* **Chapter Thirteen** *for more information about Archiving.*

Think outside the box, literally! Recipes can be found in metal, wooden or plastic card file boxes, in shoeboxes, in notebooks, in kitchen drawers, and tucked into cookbooks. They are scribbled on the backs of envelopes and included in old letters. Depending on how much time you allow yourself for this cookbook you're writing, you can explore a number of these sources and discover a great deal about your family history in the process.

Organization

When you receive recipes from your family members, mark in your notebook that that person has replied. This will help you keep track of everyone and let you know who has and has not replied. Give everyone at least two weeks before following up and contacting them a second time.

Keep the correspondence and envelope as a record of the date and address for genealogists down the road. As recipes arrive, keep them in an "in-box" in your workspace. A shoebox is good for this. Enter them into your computer document as soon as possible when they arrive (more on that in the next chapter). After the recipes have been entered, put them in your accordion file. That way you will avoid entering a recipe twice.

Checklist

Have you:
1. Contacted nearby relatives for the possibilities of borrowing their collection OR arranged a visit to go through it with them?

2. Documented the sources of the recipes?

3. Archived any old recipes you found?

4. Made a calendar or date list to remind you to contact people who have not yet replied?

5. Created an "in-box" for incoming recipes?

Chapter Four
Writing It Down
(Typing It In)

Now that you have some of the mechanics out of the way, you can *really* get started. Once you've contacted everyone, and are waiting for the recipes to start coming in, you need to set up an electronic document, and begin organizing it into the various sections. Open a new document, and give it a title. You can begin with a title page; a note of thanks from you, the author/compiler, and the Table of Contents.

Your document can be several pages long before you have entered a single recipe. By separating the sections first, it will enable you to put the recipes in the chapters they belong, and save work later on. Microsoft Word®, the program I use, has a function for forcing page breaks; it's in the pull-down menu Insert. Simply name your section at the top of the page, hit return twice, and put in a page break. If you use a different program, check your word processor's manual for inserting page breaks.

If you're not sure where to start with breaking the document into sections, go grab your favorite cookbook and see how it's arranged. My chapters were as follows: Beverages; Snacks & Hors d'Oeuvres; Bread; Sandwiches; Eggs & Cheese; Soups, Stews & Sauces; Pasta; Casseroles; Beef; Pork; Poultry; Seafood; Vegetarian; Vegetables; Salads; Cakes & Frostings; Pies; Cookies & Bars; Candies; Desserts; Helpful Hints; Index; and Recipe Contributors.

Obviously, you can exclude or include other things that are best suited for your own family. If there are lots of hunters in your family, for instance, you may want to include a "Game" chapter. Alternatively, you could have sections for "Main Dishes," "Side Dishes," "Holiday Recipes," etc. You want your cookbook to be easy to use. This is your project, arrange it as you want it. If you can't decide, get a second opinion.

Another nice thing to include are blank pages at the end of each chapter, for the person to write in new recipes, the future family favorites. You can put a header at the top of each page, something like "New Favorites" or simply leave the pages blank. The number you leave is up to you and your family. If you have avid recipe collectors in your family, three blank sheets (or six pages front and back) are not too many.

The index is a bit of a bother, but it makes the whole thing more polished, more organized and much easier to use. I entered each recipe into the index section as I went, then I added page numbers to the index last. *(More on that in Indexing.)*

With "Recipe Contributors," I listed everyone who sent a recipe. I also included family members who had died, and put their names in parentheses (or you could use italics or boldface). My reasoning was this: I wanted to attribute recipes to the people who had made them special. This is a nice way to remember family members and makes it even more precious for the next generation. Another reason is that future researchers will be able to find clues to when someone may have passed away, based on evidence presented in your cookbook.

TIP: If you choose to have a contributors page, include the maiden names of married women, *i.e.:* "Wendy (Boughner) Whipple" and birth (along with marriage and death, if applicable) years. A genealogist will thank you for it someday!

Once you have your chapters organized in a computer file, and you start receiving recipes, enter them as soon as they arrive. This is a very time-consuming activity. DO NOT put off entering them until you have a stack of them in your in-box, or you will regret it! Don't make things harder than they have to be. By entering them as you receive them, you'll stay on top of things and avoid feeling overwhelmed.

Every time you enter a recipe, a picture, or make some change to the document, *save it!* There are few things more frustrating than entering a page of text and having the power go out or your computer crash. *Save frequently!* If you live in the country and your power is a little unreliable, you might even consider buying an Uninterruptible Power Supply, or UPS. This is a box with a battery in it that goes between the outlet and your computer: if your power goes out, or just dips, it keeps the computer running and your work safe. They used to be very expensive, but you can now buy one that gives you the precious few minutes you need to save your work for well under a hundred dollars.

When you enter the recipes into the sections you have created, I recommend that you leave a space between your section header and the start of the recipes, as well as between recipes on a page. If you don't leave that space, your page will look crowded and be harder to read.

I personalized the recipe titles, *i.e.:* "Grandma Whipple's Sugar Cookies" or "Mike's Favorite Lemon Pie." Alternatively, instead of personalizing each recipe title, you could simply put the name of the person who sent you the recipe with each one: "Pecan Pie—Mabel T. Boughner." This will still enable the contributor to get the credit they deserve but will be a bit less cluttered.

After you enter each recipe, go to your index section and add the name of the recipe there, too. This will save a lot of work later. Also, if you're calling the recipe "Aunt Alice's Pickles" index it as "Pickles" or "Pickles, Aunt Alice's," or no one will be able to find anything in your index.

You may get things that aren't recipes but useful advice, like how many pounds of nuts to buy for a party, or what is the best way to get red wine stains from a tablecloth. Include those, too, and put them in a Helpful Hints section. In that section, you can also include basic information like a "hot oven" is 400°F, common substitutions, and anything else you think should be there. You could also put a key to abbreviations there.

When you enter the recipes, be sure you enter them as they were given to you. If something doesn't look right or if you don't understand an abbreviation, contact that contributor and ask. Every recipe should use the same abbreviations. You could also elect not to abbreviate at all, which will prevent any confusion or misunderstanding.

Make sure the ingredients and instructions are clear. Does the recipe call for "1 cup of pecans, chopped" or "1 cup of chopped pecans"? There's a big difference, and even though you know that the pecans are measured after they're chopped for a particular recipe, someone else who has never made that recipe might not. If you aren't certain yourself, ask the person who gave you the recipe. If something sounds wrong, and you contact the person, who then confirms that the instructions are correct, you might want to put a note in the instructions: "1 Tbsp. almond extract [yes, 1 tablespoon is the correct amount]," that will let your readers know that even though it sounds wrong, it isn't.

If it sounds as if there might be a step or two missing, contact the person who gave that recipe to you and ask. Your instructions for each recipe should be clear and explicit. If the carrot is supposed to be diced, say so. If the meat is to be seared in a bit of hot fat before you add it to the stew, say so. Cooks who use a recipe habitually will know exactly how to prepare it, but not everyone who receives a copy of your cookbook will have that same experience with every recipe. It is for everyone's benefit that each set of instructions be as complete as possible, even if it seems redundant.

Every recipe should be entered the same way, or it will be confusing to read and look sloppy. To save space and decrease the number of pages the book would be, I put the ingredients into two columns if there were more than 4 ingredients. Check the manual that came with your word processing program to see how you create columns. This is the format I chose:

"Instant" French Toast

Ingredients:

4 eggs
1 tsp. vanilla
1 C. water or milk

1 loaf of bread
cinnamon

Directions: *Save the bread wrapper!* Beat the eggs in a good-sized bowl. Add the water or milk and vanilla, and whisk until frothy. Dip bread slices in the egg mixture and place on a heated griddle. Sprinkle cinnamon on the tops before you flip them over. Set aside to cool when done. Finish with remaining bread, adding an egg and more water if necessary. When the whole loaf is done and cooled, put back into the bread wrapper, and freeze. For an "instant" breakfast, thaw the frozen pieces in a toaster (microwaving makes them mushy).

Wendy B. Whipple, Matteson, Illinois

You could also use a two-column format for the whole thing:

"Instant" French Toast
(Wendy B. Whipple)

Ingredients:

4 eggs
1 tsp. vanilla
1 C. water or milk
1 loaf of bread
cinnamon

Directions:

Save the bread wrapper! Beat the eggs with the water or milk and vanilla, and whisk until frothy. Dip bread slices in the egg mixture and place on a heated griddle. Sprinkle dipped slices with cinnamon. Set cooked slices aside to cool completely. Repeat, adding an egg and more water if necessary. When all slices have cooled, put back into the bread wrapper, and freeze. For an "instant" breakfast, thaw the frozen pieces in a toaster (microwaving makes them mushy).

Instructions can also come in the form of a numbered list.

Wendy's "Instant" French Toast

Ingredients:
4 eggs
1 tsp. vanilla
1 C. water or milk
1 loaf of bread
cinnamon

1. Beat 4 eggs with 1 C. of milk or water. Add vanilla, and whisk until frothy.
2. Heat the griddle, using low-medium heat.
3. Reserve the bread wrapper. Dip each slice of bread in the egg mixture and place on the griddle.
4. Sprinkle the bread with cinnamon.
5. Cook both sides of the bread and set aside to cool completely.
6. Repeat with remaining slices of bread, adding another egg and more liquid if needed.
7. When all the slices are cooled, put them back into the bread wrapper and freeze.
8. To serve put the desired number of slices in the toaster to thaw and heat. Do not microwave; microwaving makes the toast mushy.

There is an exception to the single format guideline. You could format it "story" style, using boldface to emphasize the ingredients:

"Instant" French Toast

Beat **4 eggs** with **1 cup of water or milk** and **1 teaspoon of vanilla**. Whisk this mixture until frothy. Heat your griddle. Take **1 loaf of bread**, saving the wrapper, and begin dipping the bread into the egg mixture. Place on the griddle, and sprinkle the tops with **cinnamon**. Turn to cook the tops, and set the cooked slices aside to cool, and repeat with the remaining slices of bread. Add another egg and more water if necessary. When all of the slices have cooled, put back into the bread wrapper and freeze. For an "instant" breakfast, thaw the frozen pieces in a toaster (microwaving makes them mushy) and serve.

Contributed by Wendy B. Whipple

Since most of the recipes you receive will be in a more typical format, this style could be used occasionally when you receive recipes that have no set instructions. If you are talking to family members about the dishes they cook, you could write down (or record with a tape recorder) what they say, and include that word-for-word in a format like this. This is an especially effective way to include those cooking stories. It has the effect of listening to a person tell you how to make something, rather than simply reading directions. Keep in mind that an entire book written this way will be more of a memoir than a useable cookbook.

There are many ways to write a recipe. Just be sure you are consistent throughout your cookbook. If you're having trouble deciding how you want to format yours, pick up your favorite cookbook (one you use often), and see how it's formatted.

I preferred not to have recipes split onto two pages, and rearranged them on the pages (cutting and pasting) so that they fit on the pages as efficiently as possible. (One long recipe on a page with a short one, etc.) I used page breaks to force the next page when all that rearranging wasn't enough. If you don't mind recipes overlapping onto the next page, you will avoid that extra work, but keep in mind that it is inconvenient to have to turn the page mid-recipe. Some sources advocate putting a single recipe on a page, and using illustrations, quotes, or helpful hints to fill in any blank spaces left by shorter recipes. If the size of your book is going to be 5.5 x 8.5 inches (sheets of 8.5 x 11 folded over), that is certainly an option, but for an 8.5-x-11-inch book, that's wasting a lot of space, and increasing your costs.

When you begin to receive recipes, check to see if the card or page says whom it's from. If it does not, write that notation on it *in pencil* (the ink in most pens can cause damage to the card over time). Documenting sources is critical when doing research, but it's also nice for a project like this, when a genealogist may come across your papers, and gain important information from them. And because you were thorough enough to take a minute to note that the Deviled Egg recipe was from your great-aunt Lila Smith, and to keep the envelope she sent it in, the researcher will know who she was, what her relationship to you and the rest of the family was, and where she lived. Even if you personally are not interested in genealogy, your child, your cousin, or some other family member might be in the future. Someday, someone will thank you for being so thorough!

Keep every recipe that is sent to you. It may not be an heirloom now, but in 20 years it will be! Recipes are little bits of family ephemera, precious for the fact that it's a record of not only the recipe, but also a family member's handwriting. If you borrow a recipe collection from someone, color-photocopy any cards that may be getting fragile with wear. If you have the ability to do so, scan them, and burn the files on a CD to save indefinitely.

If cards are scanned, and they're hard to read because of fading ink or yellowing paper, a graphics program like Photoshop® will help you adjust the color and contrast so that a barely legible card is once again useable. (But that's a whole other book!) MS Word® has some limited capabilities for adjusting an image's color and contrast.

Page Numbers

If your word processor has a command for inserting page numbers, be sure you make use of it. There's no point in indexing if you don't have the page numbers on the pages.

If you can't insert page numbers (or you forgot to put them in before you printed it out), then you can carefully handwrite those numbers on the pages. This is obviously not a good option if you printed several copies. You could use stickers on the pages with the appropriate numbers on them, if you're only printing a couple of copies, or are printing a single original and making photocopies of the original. Places selling scrapbook supplies usually have a huge array of stickers to choose from. Keep in mind that if you're photocopying in black and white, colored stickers will be in shades of gray. A cute red heart sticker with the number 5 in the middle is going to look black in a black and white photocopy.

Organization

By now, you should have a document file on your computer, organized into the sections you have chosen. Keep recipes that you have entered separate from those you have not. Note recipes that aren't immediately identified with a name, and write that information on them. *Remember to save your document frequently!*

Checklist

Have you:

1. Created your electronic document?

2. Separated the chapters?

3. Noted whom the recipes are from, if not immediately identifiable?

4. Begun entering recipes as they arrive?

5. Verified any unclear instructions?

6. Added the recipes to the index, alphabetizing as you go?

7. Added the page numbers?

Chapter Five
Making It Personal

Chances are if you are going to the trouble of writing a family cookbook, you want to include information about your family members. After all, a cookbook without all those people and stories is just a collection of recipes. Add the family history, and you have an *heirloom*. What makes your book precious is its connection to your family, a window into *your* past. And please don't believe that if you don't have generations mapped back to the Mayflower or you're not descended from George Washington, you don't have any family history! Whether it's two generations or twenty, your family's story is worth telling.

When you visit or call your family members, ask about the recipes, ask how they learned to cook, invite them to tell you stories about the kitchen garden or going fishing early in the morning. Make sure you take plenty of notes; don't rely on your memory to keep things straight when you get back to your computer to type it all in. Some of this information could be used in the form of short biographies about each contributor, but don't limit yourself only to contributors, or your cookbook's family history element may be horribly one sided in that many of your contributors will likely be the women, leaving the men out of your history.

Don't ask closed-end questions, questions that can be answered with a single word, like "Did Grandma Wilma teach you to cook?" Ask instead, "How did you learn to cook?" You may find it helpful to have a list of questions you want to ask, but don't stick to your list rigidly. The responses you get to one question may inspire six more (as you take notes, jot down those other questions so you won't forget to ask). Pay attention to the person you're talking to. If you're only looking down at your notes while you write or ask the questions, the person won't be nearly as likely to open up to you, and share their life. Be a considerate listener and don't interrupt. If you don't understand something, ask for a clarification. You might also consider tape-(or video-)recording the interview, if that person is comfortable doing so. You would then have a record of someone's voice as well as their stories for future generations.

Here are some questions that might help get you started:

- How did you learn to cook? How old were you?
- What is one of the first things you remember making?
- What were things people requested you make?
- What were you most proud of? Most embarrassed by?
- What recipes was your mother known for?
- What was your father's role in cooking and mealtimes?
- What was your grandparents' (maternal and paternal) ethnic food heritage?
- What kinds of food did you eat at their house?
- What kind of holiday recipes do you remember? When were they served, who made them?
- What other family member's recipes do you recall?
- What was dinnertime like? When did you eat? Was it "supper" or "dinner?"
- What kinds of things were the favorites of the children (yours, or when you were a child)?
- What traditions were there for birthdays (especially the birthday cake)?
- How did your family celebrate or entertain? What kinds of things were served?
- Who did you exchange recipes with, and what were they?
- Did you make gifts from the kitchen? If so, what were they?
- What is your favorite cookbook? Why?
- What special dishes, silverware or linens are important to the family?
- What stories do you know about those heirlooms?

Interesting things often come up in casual conversation. My mother recently told me that her mother never had many cookbooks (probably because her mother taught her to cook), and that the books she did have were lost in a fire. If she had many handwritten recipes before the fire, she didn't have any afterwards. That dates the recipes I have of Grandma's as being written after 1973, when they had the fire. (I have gotten into the habit of carrying a small notebook in my purse, for just those occasions when something of historical significance is mentioned.)

One thing that you should be very careful of is family legends. Most families have stories that get told and retold, sometimes growing as they're told again and again. Legends should not be reported as fact unless they are verifiable. It's fine to retell some of those marvelous stories, so long as you make it clear that it may be only a story. The reason for this is that a few generations from now, someone may be reading your cookbook and come across a tidbit they believe to be fact, when it may not be. If that person is a genealogist, that bit of misinformation could send them down a wrong path for months or years of flawed research.

Some recipes may have particular memories attached to them, or they might have an explanation that's not readily apparent. For instance, why did Great-Grandma Martin have so many recipes that fed a dozen people, when her family wasn't that large? Perhaps she was a farm wife, and the recipes were for cooking for the farm laborers. Perhaps even though her immediate family wasn't large, she had extended family living with her. Perhaps she was very active in the church and those dinners were made after services, when several parishioners joined her family for dinner every Sunday. Do a little digging. You will likely find things you never knew about your family, and will be able to preserve your findings for generations to come.

Stories can be told in the place that they fit best. In my section on pies, I included three generations of stories about pie disasters. My grandmother once made a pie for my Uncle Mike for Christmas (his favorite, lemon), but she left out the sugar! Mom once made a cherry pie for a neighbor for his birthday, but she forgot to remove the cherry stones (he gave her a cherry pitter as a gift soon thereafter).

43

I made a sweet potato pie (something I'd never made before) for a good friend of ours. The recipe called for bourbon, but after 2 hours of cooking, the bourbon still hadn't cooked out. So long as everyone has a good sense of humor, telling those stories isn't hurtful. And that's something to keep in mind: if family members don't like a particular story told about them because they find it embarrassing or hurtful, don't tell it. Just because it happened doesn't mean it has to be told over and over, and immortalized in your book.

You also don't have to limit yourself to stories involving cooking and food. Your cookbook will be more than a means to make Grandma's best cookies: it will be a way to preserve generations of history. Ask for the stories, and then let people tell them in their own words. If you're talking to people, this is where it's very helpful to use a tape recorder. If they are responding with stories they mail to you, transcribe them word for word. By letting your family members tell the stories rather than paraphrasing them yourself, you preserve those voices that future generations would not otherwise have heard.

Historical "Trivia"

I added historical information about various family members' birth years at the end of each chapter. The web site "On This Day In History..." is great source for this: see http://www.dmarie.com/timecap/. For instance, when I was born in 1970, Richard M. Nixon was president, a loaf of bread was 24¢, *Bridge Over Troubled Water* was a popular song, and *Patton* won the Academy Award for Best Picture. This will enable future generations to get an idea of what life was like "back then." It's not absolutely necessary, but it's a fun way to review history and make it meaningful.

Family Trees

With the help of a genealogy program that will print out family trees, this part is easy. If you don't have a genealogy program that will do this, there are places online to get pedigree sheets you can fill out by hand. The Latter Day Saints website, http://www.familysearch.org, has many forms you can use. Check http://www.cyndislist.com/supplies.htm for more sources for charts and other supplies. There are also scrapbook pages that have spaces for filling in pedigrees. Fan charts are a very space-efficient way to get lots of names on a small page.

Using pedigrees in your cookbook will not only help other family members keep track of who's who, but will also be a valuable legacy for future generations. You needn't go back seven generations to make it meaningful, but if you have several generations of recipe contributors, include them all.

Biographies

Another way to approach this idea is to include short biographies for each of the contributors. Instead of your contributors page merely being a list of names, list the name and then a little bit about the person. For example:

Wendy Boughner Whipple

Wendy was born in Danville, Illinois. She grew up in Fithian, IL, and attended Oakwood High School. She went to Drake University in Des Moines, Iowa, where she met her husband-to-be, Marc. They graduated and got married in 1992, and their daughter Diana was born in 1997.

It doesn't need to be fancy or elaborate, just a few lines about the person and their family. If you have photos of all your contributors (and if you don't you can probably get them), you could include a small photograph of the person as well. (Remember, using black and white photos will help keep your printing costs down.) It might be helpful to have a list of questions that you ask of each contributor, so that you will have consistent information from everyone: Where were you born, where you grew up, when you married your spouse, etc.

If you have a contributors section of your cookbook with the biographical information, you could also list the page numbers of their recipes:

Wilma Shunk Kelly Offutt (1921-1991)

Wilma was born in Freedom, Indiana. She married twice, once to Edward Kelly (whom she divorced), and then to Everett Offutt. She had three children: Sharon with Edward, and Mike and Paul with Everett. She loved to travel and did so when she was not working in her home office as a bookkeeper. *6, 31, 46, 56, 61, 65*

Recipe Comments

Another way to add historical/biographical information to your cookbook is to include with recipes comments that people have made about those recipes. For instance, this is what my mother-in-law had to say about the marvelous dinner rolls she makes at Thanksgiving and Christmas: "I started years ago trying to make rolls like Grandma Grim made—they were so light. I've never duplicated their light texture, but I keep trying." With that single comment, she reveals that Grandma Grim had a gift when it came to those rolls. (Incidentally, my mother-in-law's rolls are phenomenally good—I can only imagine what her grandmother's rolls tasted like!)

Another thing to consider when you're reading someone else's notes or hearing their comments is that what may be common knowledge to you and your family *now* may not be commonly known a generation into the future. If something obscure is mentioned, be sure that you know what the meaning is, and include an editorial comment of your own: "Dad always brought Mom chocolate-covered cherries [for Christmas], and he loved the ribbon candy." The comment [for Christmas] is my own insertion, to clarify what my aunt meant. Similarly, slang (current or from earlier times) should have notes explaining the word or phrase. If you get comments or notes from someone that you're not sure of the meaning or significance, *ask.*

> TIP: Try to keep in mind that not everyone in your family knows what you know. You've done the research; you've talked to the people. It's your job now to share that knowledge in such a way that future generations will

understand. Try to look at the information you have compiled from an outsider's viewpoint. If you come to a statement that is unclear, like mention of a family ritual that everyone (living) knows about, be more explicit so that someday, a great-great-grandchild or nephew or distant cousin will also know about that ritual, even if it is no longer practiced.

These are just a few examples of how taking an extra step or two can make your cookbook very special and utterly priceless to the people who receive it, and the generation they will pass it down to. This information is the sort that genealogists pray to find: clues into relationships and history, facts otherwise clouded by time.

Crediting a Contributor

Just as there are many formats a recipe can use, there are many ways to credit the contributors of recipes. One way would be to make their name part of the title of the recipe: "Sharon's Egg Salad," for example. The problem with that is that not everyone will know who Sharon is, especially a generation or two down the road. Another option is to have the title of the recipe, and then the name of the contributor: "Egg Salad, Sharon O. Boughner." The name of the recipe could be on one side of the page and the contributor's name at the other side—the easiest way to do this would be to just use the TAB key to move the name to the proper location. A third alternative is to have the contributor's name at the end of the recipe. If you use only the contributor's first and last name, consider including their maiden name (where applicable) in a separate contributors list. See the previous chapter (the section on recipe formats) for examples of some of the ways you can give credit where credit is due. If your family is far-flung, why not also include where they're living at the time that they made their contribution? This is one more little thing that may really help a family historian as they trace the migration of family members. It's a step that may not seem significant now, but in twenty years or more it may be the clue someone really needed to make a connection.

It's possible that the same recipe will be contributed by more than one person. Crazy Cake, Wacky Cake and Depression Cake are all names for a particular eggless recipe mixed right in the pan that it's baked in. Lots of folks have that in their recipe collection. If you get the same recipe submitted by more than one person, make certain everyone gets credited. If the same recipe has title variations, you might choose one and put the rest of the names at the end of the recipe, "also known as:" and be sure you use each of those names in the index, since different people may know the recipe by different names.

By using a contributors index, you can also keep all the recipes from a given individual together. It doesn't have to be a biographical format, but just an alphabetical list of the contributors (remember to include maiden names, where applicable), and the pages on which their recipes appear—*see* **Chapter Eight, Indexing,** *for examples*. This will not take the place of including the name of the person with the recipes, however, so be sure you don't leave that out. Your method of crediting individuals can be as elaborate or succinct as you prefer, just remember to be consistent from person to person and from recipe to recipe.

Ethnic Heritage

Many of us can lay claim to a wealth of ethnic identities. Americans in particular have a very varied cultural identity, but we certainly have no monopoly on that. If your family is ethnically diverse, celebrate it! If you know when your great-great-grandparents arrived in the New World, that's a wonderful thing to include somewhere in your cookbook. Family history is incomplete without those pieces, along with the other, more localized information. Even if you don't have a recipe from that long-ago immigrant, their heritage lives on in your family. Without telling your family's story in a medium as permanent as a book, you risk those stories being forgotten forever. Any opportunity you have to preserve your history should be enthusiastically embraced.

It's not necessary to turn your cookbook into a history book. This is, after all, not a memoir, but a cookbook. If you have a recipe for sauerkraut from Grandma Smith, who is a third-generation German-American, that affords the opportunity to mention that Grandma Smith's great-grandmother came to America in 1798 with her parents on the ship *Anne Marie*. Chances are good that not everyone in the family knows about that detail, so by sharing it with everyone, you've enriched everyone's own personal history.

Native Language(s)

If your family has a collection of recipes that are in a language (or languages) other than English, consider including them, too, along with their translation. This helps preserve one more facet of your ethnic heritage. If your family is bilingual, you may want to include the entire cookbook in both languages. It will be twice the work, but it will make everyone in the family, from naturalized immigrants who may not be fluent in English to the school children who may barely speak the language of their great-grandparents, comfortably able to use your cookbook. This will create such a treasure for future generations!

Organization

As you gather your family stories and write them down, or enter them into your computer, be sure to record the name of the person who told the story and when, and whether or not it can be verified. Decide what information to include if you're going to have brief biographies of people, and be consistent with everyone. If you use historical trivia, keep those notes handy, so they can be inserted throughout the book. If you have recipe comments, make sure that they get put in with the right recipes.

Checklist

Have you:

1. Gathered family stories and recorded the source information?

2. Verified facts and noted which might be legends?

3. Collected the biographical information?

4. Collected the historical information?

5. Double-checked to be certain that the comments match the recipes?

6. Double-checked the comments for clarity and made notes of your own in the text to clarify any obscure or old-fashioned references?

Chapter Six
About Fonts

Typefaces can be a lot of fun to play with. Keep in mind, however, that some decorative fonts can be very hard to read, and more than two type styles in one document is visually distracting. Stick with a single, easy to read font for your recipes, and another font to use as an accent. I used Arial for the main font and Lucida Handwriting for my accent. By "main font," I mean the typeface that will comprise the body of the cookbook, what the recipes and notations will use. By "accent font," I mean the typeface that is more decorative, appearing as chapter titles or other small places, as with the alphabet headings in the index.

There are a vast number of fonts available to the average computer-user, many free for download, and there's sure to be one that suits you and your project perfectly. You will want to choose a typeface that fits in with your chosen theme or mood of your cookbook. There are fonts that are very casual (like Lucida Handwriting), and some that are very formal. A very classic-looking typeface may look stuffy if the overall tone of your book is open and chatty. Conversely, a really casual font will look strange if you are presenting the book with a serious or historical tone. If done well, most likely no one will notice that your chosen typeface reflects the mood of your cookbook. Done poorly, your fonts will be jarring and obvious, even if no one can quite tell why. Careful consideration to this small detail can make a good cookbook a great one.

When you're producing something that is made for reading by others, simplicity is always your best option. Yes, there are some wonderful flashy fonts, and you can alter them further in graphics programs with all kinds of fill tricks or by distorting text. Just remember that people are going to be *using* this cookbook. It's not a poster that has to get someone's attention, so keep it simple, and it will be a pleasure to use.

Keep in mind the people who will be receiving copies of your cookbook. If many people are having trouble with their eyesight, consider using a slightly larger size type. Even increasing the size a couple of points can help. Vision impairment is another reason to use easy-to-read fonts, since many decorative fonts can be difficult to read. Whatever size you choose, *be consistent*. If you use a certain size for the body text on one page, use it throughout. All your chapter titles should be the same size as well.

Chapter titles should be a larger size than the rest of your document, especially if you don't plan to use artwork to separate your sections. This will help people flipping through your cookbook find what they are looking for. The book will be more organized if the sections are clearly defined.

Avoid typing long lines in all capital letters. As you can see, TYPING IN ALL CAPS IS HARD TO READ FOR MORE THAN A FEW WORDS. (And for those people who are used to online communications, typing in all caps is the virtual equivalent of shouting.) You may choose to use **boldface** for the titles of recipes, or use a slightly larger size. You could use those options in combination, as well. By making your recipe titles stand out, you will increase the amount of differentiation from recipe to recipe. I used boldface for my recipe titles.

Boldface and italic text should not be overused. Both will lose their emphasis if used without regard to style and substance. If you're inserting your own notes into recipes, you can use [square brackets] or *italics* to indicate an editorial remark. Italics can also be used to indicate direct quotations; *Mama made this for us whenever we were home sick.* Recipe comments from your contributors can be italicized instead of enclosing them in quotation marks. Bold type can be used to separate sections of a recipe (ingredients list, directions), or to indicate a warning, such as **This recipe cannot be doubled.** Because computers can do both italic and boldface text, the use of underlines is unnecessary and can make text hard to read by interfering with the "descenders," those parts of the letters which fall below the line of text: g, p, y, etc.

If color is an option (and this will affect the cost of printing), black type is going to be the highest contrast on most paper, even if your paper isn't white. Some of the cookbook publishers offer colored ink as an add-on, usually green, red, brown or blue. Those are darker shades of those colors, however, and if you print your cookbook yourself, you should keep that in mind. For instance, navy blue will have much higher contrast than turquoise.

Besides style, size, and color, there is another thing to consider when you are putting text to paper. You don't want your recipes or other text to end with a single word or small phrase on the following page. It breaks up the text and unnecessarily interrupts reading. If you have one of those situations, you can deal with it by editing the text, or by putting in a page break to move the entire recipe to the next page. The latter solution can lead to lots of unused paper (and end up costing more to print due to an increased number of pages), so your best option is editing.

One way to edit your text so that you don't have one of those "orphaned" words is to hyphenate some of your lines. By hyphenating some of the longer words that won't all fit at the end of one line, you will decrease little by little the number of lines the text takes up. The proper way to hyphenate is to separate the words by syllable. Kneading would be knead-ing, condensed would be condensed, etc. You can also rephrase some of the text to get the same result, but if you are copying someone's directions word for word, that isn't always the best way to go. You will have to decide whether you are editing your contributors' recipes for clarity and content, or if you are using their words exactly. My suggestion is that you edit for clarity/content only in the recipe instructions. If they have comments that go with the recipe, such as "This freezes well," or "We always served this for Easter brunch," quote them as they were written without changing their words.

Another way to avoid orphans is to turn off "justified" margins if you have it on. Justified text is when both the left and right margins are straight. Justified left is the easiest to read, and if you also have the right side justified, your computer will create larger gaps between words as it adjusts the spacing to eliminate a ragged right margin. Most professionally published books and newspapers are justified, because by hyphenating many of the words, the amount of words on the page or in the column is greater. Lots of hyphenated words, or large gaps between them, will make your text harder to read.

Organization

If you don't have fonts installed on your computer that you want to use, there are many websites that have free fonts to download. Simply do a search with any search engine, and look for "free fonts." Once you've downloaded them, you have to install them. Many of the font websites will also contain information on how to install the font into your system, if you don't already know how.

Checklist

Have you:

1. Chosen the font(s) you want to use?

2. Considered how the kind of font will affect the tone of your book?

3. Decided on the best size?

4. Considered what color you want the print to be?

5. Checked for orphaned words or phrases, and made any needed changes?

6. Turned off "justified" margins?

Chapter Seven
Adding Art

You may want to use clipart for your cookbook, whether it is something to illustrate each chapter heading, as section dividers, or to add to individual recipes. The art you choose can be black and white or in color. Just be aware that your printing costs will be higher if you use color. (This is true even if—or especially if—you print it at home with your own ink.)

As with fonts, it's best to keep things simple. Too many illustrations on a page will be distracting from the text and draw attention away from what the book really is: a cookbook. Every recipe does not need its own illustration. By choosing your images selectively, whether they are clipart or photos, you will enhance the look of your text without distracting from it.

Clipart and photos can also convey a particular style. You will want to choose art that is in keeping with the tone you have set with your writing style and chosen font(s). Cartoonish clipart is abundantly available, but that doesn't lend itself to a book with a historical theme. Likewise, many old-fashioned silhouettes are very elegant and may not suit the tone of a baby-shower-themed cookbook. If your collection of photographs is largely formal portrait-style, try to stick with that. If you have a lot of candid snapshots, use that as your dominant style. This is yet another way that you can make your cookbook very polished in a way that no one will notice, unless you choose a style not in keeping with the tone you have set.

Choosing Clipart

Dover Publishing has series of books of royalty-free clipart that you can scan and use, and some of their books come with CD-ROMs—no scanning! Some of their titles include: *Ready-to-Use Food and Drink Spot Illustrations, Ready-to-Use Gourmet Food Illustrations* and *Ready-to-Use Humorous Food Shopping Illustrations*, as well as other themes. Most bookstores stock these books and can order what they don't have on hand, or you can order directly from Dover's website: http://www.doverpublications.com.

If you do use clipart, use a "family" of art, something that comes in a set, so that all the pictures will have the same look and feel to them. For instance, some of Dover's clipart includes old-fashioned silhouettes. If you were to use some of those for part of your cookbook, then use some full-color modern, stylized graphic, they wouldn't "go" together and would distract from your cookbook, rather than enhance it. Being selective with your art, like using fonts selectively, will keep your book from being too cluttered. The exceptions to this are family-drawn illustrations and photographs. Enlisting the aid of a family artist (or artists) is a wonderful way to include young family members in your project. Scan these artworks and label the backs with the name of the artist, and the date. Keep those drawings with the recipes you receive in your file in a safe place.

Choosing Photographs

If your family has a sizable collection of photos, you could use scanned copies of photos to personalize the book, and put the photos on the contributors page, in a separate "photo album," or with individual recipes. Some day in the future, a child could open your cookbook and not only find that cherished recipe from their great-great-grandmother, but see a picture of her as well. You see, you really are creating an heirloom!

If you are using current photos or are taking them yourself, try to take people's pictures against a neutral and simple background. Otherwise you might end up with photographs that have cluttered backgrounds that detract from the person or persons in the picture.

The backgrounds don't need to be a blank wall, just something without a lot of other things in it. Kitchen photos with people cooking are nice if the lighting is good, and there aren't a lot of other people standing around.

If you have a digital camera, use it. That will make cropping the photos and adjusting the contrast or brightness easy. Cropping can take out some of the background clutter, and adjusting brightness may make up for a poorly lit room. Be careful not to crop too closely to the person in the photo, or they will look "crowded" by the edges of the picture. Don't overdo the exposure correction, making a too-bright photo grayish, or a too-dark photo washed out. Be aware that color photos when converted to grayscale don't look the same. If you're using black and white photos, set your camera to black and white if you're able.

It's best to use photos that are all close to the same size. Little photos can be scanned at a higher resolution and enlarged, and large photos can be reduced. Pick a size and try to be consistent. It's one more design tactic that will be unnoticeable if done right, and jarring if not.

Recipes for Illustrations

If you have old recipes that you have scanned for preservation, you can also use them as illustrations in your cookbook. Just make sure that they are sized to be readable, with any contrast adjustments as needed. It will be helpful to type out the recipe you've scanned, especially if the original is difficult to read even after doctoring from a graphics editor. A transcription of the recipe, with clarifications, will help others duplicate the recipe. For instance, many older recipes may refer to a "hot oven." You may know, but others might not, that a hot oven is 400 degrees Fahrenheit.

If you have a graphics program loaded on your computer but aren't very familiar with it, now is a great time to learn. Not only is it important from a legibility viewpoint, when you're adding all those recipes as graphics to your cookbook, but also from an archival point of view. The older those pages and cards get, the more they will degrade with time. What is hard to read now might be impossible to read in five years.

Inserting Art

I chose color pictures that were about 3 inches square as chapter headers. You could use larger pictures and separate each chapter with a full-size image. I used art *only* for the beginnings of chapters, choosing not to use any clipart for individual recipes. That is totally your choice. Keep in mind that some publishing options are only available in black and white, or that full-color publishing might be prohibitively expensive.

Microsoft Word® has an "insert art" command, which makes it very simple to insert art into your computer document. Check your manual for instructions on doing this in other programs.

You will make things much easier for yourself if you put all the electronic art, whether you're using illustrations or photos, in one folder on your computer, so they're easy to find. In that folder, you should have all the art you want to use, whether it's scanned clipart or images you downloaded. You might also consider renaming the image files so you know where they go without having to look at them every time. *I.e.:* Your illustrations for the section on cookies could be called "cookies.jpg" (or -.gif or -.tif). Or, if you are illustrating with family photos, try using the family member's initials or first name to help you choose the image you want from a folder full of image files.

If your word processing program does not have this function, simply take the art you want to use, in the size you need (enlarging or reducing as needed), and use low-tack, repositionable glue (3M makes Post-It® glue that is perfect for this, much neater than rubber cement) to put the illustration on the page you've printed out. You will need to leave space in your document for the art to go when it's printed out. Once a copy is made of that page, it will be your master for the other copies you need to make.

After every image you add (and every recipe you add), save the document! *And save frequently!* In fact, you might also consider saving your work-in-progress to a disk, especially when you're getting ready to print, or to have it printed.

Color vs. Black and White

Printing in full color is more expensive than printing in black and white. If you're only planning on making a few copies, that's not as much of an issue as it is if you're printing fifty. Color photocopies from a retail copying business may cost as much as ten times more than black and white. Buying color ink cartridges for your printer isn't cheap, either. Cost aside, it will also impact your book if you have illustrations that are color *and* black and white. Consider sticking with one or the other. Photos are the exception. Obviously, old photos are going to be in black and white, and most people take pictures of their families today with color film.

Something else to consider when it comes to art and paper color: If you use a paper color other than white, it will change the way those images appear on the page, since most printer ink is not opaque. If you're using black and white or grayscale images, it's not really an issue. As an example, if your image has yellow in it, and you're printing on pink paper, the resulting art is going to look orangey. The same image converted to grayscale would look fine on any color paper. (Word® has a function to convert images to grayscale, under Format–Picture. If you are using a graphics program, check your manual for how to do this.)

Organization

Any art for your cookbook should be in one place. If you're using scanned art, consider marking on the back of the original *lightly and in pencil* where the art is to be placed. Artwork from the children in the family (or adults) should similarly be marked, along with the artist's name. Keep all of those pieces of art in your accordion file, with your letters and recipes.

Electronic artwork should be kept in a single folder on your computer. If necessary, make notations in your notebook or in another computer document, which images go where in the book. *I.e.:* "veggies.jpg" goes at the beginning of your section on vegetable dishes.

Checklist

Have you:

1. Chosen the artwork you want to use?

2. Is the artwork from the same "family" of art?

3. Is the artwork consistent with the tone you have set with your writing style, format, and font selections?

4. Have you decided on color vs. black and white?

5. If you're using photos, have they all been similarly sized?

6. Are the images scanned and in a single folder on your computer?

7. Are the images renamed so you know what image goes where?

8. Are the physical copies of your art in your accordion file, labeled with the artist's name (where applicable)?

Chapter Eight
Indexing

Once all the recipes are entered and the art is in place, you can begin your indexing. Hopefully, you have already added the various recipes to the index without page numbers. If so, all you will have to do is check page numbers and add them.

One thing I highly recommend once the pictures are inserted (if you use any), is to take a notebook and list the recipes with the page they're on. Then you can go to your index and enter those page numbers, crossing them off your list as you go. That will save you a lot of back-and-forth in your document; it's an extra step, but one that will end up saving you time.

When you set up your index page(s), it's wise to go ahead and use all the letters of the alphabet. If you don't have any X or Q recipes, you can delete those letters when you're done, but you'll at least have the letters there in case you get a recipe for Quince Jelly. To conserve paper, I put my index in two columns. See your manual for how to make columns with your word processor.

The quickest way to index is to alphabetize the recipes by name with their page number. When you enter recipes into the index, simplify the titles. As mentioned before, a recipe you call "Aunt Alice's Pickles" is probably not what your readers will look for in the index. They will look for a pickle recipe under P. If you want to differentiate between recipes with the same name, you can use something like this:

Tuna Casserole, Beth O., 31
Tuna Casserole, Wendy W., 30

The next degree of complexity in an index would be to categorize the kind of recipe, and then alphabetize the categories: Appetizers, Beverages, Desserts, Main Dishes, Side Dishes, etc., and then to alphabetize within the category:

> *DESSERTS*
> *Apple Pudding,* 80
> *Baklava,* 83
> *Caramel Apple Cobbler,* 81

Some cookbooks will index a recipe under several variations of its title:

> *Apple Cobbler, Caramel,* 81
> *Caramel Apple Cobbler,* 81
> *Cobbler, Caramel Apple,* 81

If you receive recipes that have name variations, be sure to index all of those variations, since some people will know it by different names, and look for it in your index accordingly:

> *Crazy Cake,* 54
> *Depression Cake,* 54
> *Wacky Cake,* 54

You could also choose to index recipes by their contributor:

> Boughner, Sharon
> > *Cheese Balls,* 19
> > *Egg Salad,* 18
> > *Sugar Cookies,* 73
> Boughner, Tom Jr.
> > *Lasagna,* 26
> > *Taco Pie,* 29

As you can see, your index can be as elaborate or as simple as you want, and there are many variations on the theme. If you're really feeling detail oriented, you could even include more than one index—the first organized by recipe name, the second by contributor, for example. Keep in mind that the more complex your index, the longer it will take to do.

If you choose to do an extensive index, write each recipe in your notebook (or on an index card), and list the other places in the index that it should appear. After everything's entered, write the page number that the recipe is on. When you start to type up the index, you can refer to your notes to index the book. That will speed things along nicely, since you won't have to go back and forth within your document, getting the page numbers. (Which is how I did it...and what a pain it was!)

Indexing is tedious, but it will be worth it when you're done. A few times, I considered stopping and skipping the index altogether, it was such an ordeal. I am so glad I kept up and finished the index, because as much as I refer to my cookbook, it makes it a lot handier to use.

Some word processing programs have indexing features. It may be worth your time to learn to use that function if your cookbook is a large one, or if you plan on making more cookbooks in the future.

Don't forget to have your proofreader(s) check your index pagination, and make sure that the index accurately guides your readers to the right pages.

Some of the cookbook publishers (*see* **Chapter Eleven**) will do the indexing for you. If you use one of them, and they do the indexing, rejoice! They're saving you a real chore. Be sure you check if it is an option you have to pay for, or if they include indexing in their standard options. It may be worth it to you to have an index, even if you have to pay a little extra.

Organization

The best way to stay organized with the index is to enter the recipes into it as soon as you've entered it into the body of the cookbook, alphabetizing as you go. The next best way is to make a list of recipes after they have all been entered, and note what page they're on. When you update the index with page numbers, you won't have to scroll up and down in your document to find the page numbers.

Checklist

Have you:

1. Set up your index with all 26 letters of the alphabet? (Or with the letters of the alphabet you're using, if not the Roman alphabet?)

2. Decided on the organization type and level of complexity your index will have?

3. Used a notebook or note cards to write down the recipes and page numbers?

4. Entered the recipes into the index after entering them into their sections?

Chapter Nine
Proofreading

Before you print the final draft, have someone else proofread it, preferably more than one person. It can be hard to see your own mistakes, so a fresh pair of eyes is helpful. Running a spell checker helps, but it won't pick up every error. I'm still finding mistakes in my cookbook that could have been avoided if someone had proofread it for me. One particularly embarrassing error: A recipe for tuna casserole has no tuna listed in the ingredients, and it was my own recipe! A candy recipe doesn't include the butter required to make it. These are avoidable mistakes; have someone proofread your cookbook.

TIP: If you're not certain about a recipe's ingredients or instructions, be sure to follow up with the person who sent it to you.

Here are things for your proofreader(s) to check for:

1. Clarity (Are the directions understandable?)

2. Spelling errors

3. Grammatical errors

4. Ingredient omissions

5. Typos in the amounts and temperatures (Have them mark anything that doesn't look right, so you can double-check it against the original.)

6. Pagination and page breaks

7. Accuracy in the index.

Print out a copy for your proofreader to read, and give them a colored pencil or pen to make their notations for corrections or clarifications. Once they have given the corrected copy back, make your corrections, and print a fresh copy and have a second person review it. Make the needed corrections, and have the first person read it again, or enlist a third person. This will be the best way to ensure that your final draft will have as few errors in it as possible.

The correcting and proofing can take as long as you want it to. You can keep passing corrected copies back and forth until no one can find any errors at all, or you can trust that twice is enough. Since you're the one with the deadline, it's up to you to decide how long this process will take.

This is a really underappreciated task. It's tedious, certainly, but necessary if you want your cookbook to be clear and accurate. If your proofreaders are as enthusiastic about your project as you are, it won't be such a chore for them. But don't forget to thank them!

Organization

Once you have a hard copy in someone's hands for proofing, ask a second person if they will do the same when you get the book back. Make the corrections, print out a fresh copy, and have the second person proofread it. Ask your proofreaders to have the copy back to you in a reasonable amount of time; a week (per person) may be enough time unless it is a particularly long cookbook. That way, you can get corrections made, and have it re-proofed, and re-corrected if necessary, in three weeks or less.

Checklist

Have you:

1. Printed a hard copy?

2. Asked someone to proofread for you?

3. Informed them what to look for

4. Made the first round of corrections?

5. Printed a corrected copy for the second proofreader?

6. Made the second set of corrections?

Chapter Ten
Committing It to Paper

You're almost finished. You've got your cookbook all put together, you've had it proofread, and you've checked your index pagination. This is where you either print it out yourself, a fine option if you're only making a few copies, or take it to a local printer and have them print and bind it for you. If you already have the means to bind it, then you can also have the printer just make the copies you need, and save money for binding and collating.

Paper

Paper is an important consideration, whether you print the book yourself or have it printed by a copy shop or publisher. Printers often have a variety of paper colors to choose from, and there are many, many options available for your desktop printer at home. If possible, use acid-free paper; it will last longer. Be careful with your color choices. While using bright, fluorescent paper might seem like a good idea at the time, you're almost certain to cause eyestrain and headaches for everyone using your cookbook. Pastels are a much better choice if you're going to use color. There are even pastel variety packs with 5 different colors in them. You could use them to differentiate your sections.

What "weight" of paper will you use? Copier paper is 20-lb. bond, but 24-lb. is a better choice because it's thicker and not as see-through. It's also more expensive. "Multipurpose" 20-lb. can run from $4 to $7 for a ream (500 sheets) depending on who the manufacturer is. The thicker 24-lb. can run from $6 to $10 per ream. It's usually cheaper to buy a case of paper, with either 5 or 10 reams to the case, if you will be needing that much paper. Don't forget to check and see if acid-free paper is available. It will say if it is on the package.

Specialty papers are also nice to use, but can be prohibitively expensive: more than $20 per pack of 100, comparable to buying individual sheets of scrapbook paper. Unlike scrapbook paper, you can buy large quantities of the same style easily.

If you're only making a few copies, printing at home is certainly an option, but also time consuming if you're going to use double-sided pages. If you're making a large number of copies, take it to a printer/copier and have them make the copies for you; they often have volume discounts. Depending on costs in your area, double-sided photocopies will run around 16¢ a page (8¢ a side) for black and white copies. Color copies are about a dollar per page, unless you get into volume discounts. Call and find out if having a printer make your copies is affordable for your budget. Have the number of pages you need copied with you when you call, so you can get an accurate quote. Keep all those price quotes together in your notebook, and note who has the best price.

Themed papers with borders are pretty, but usually quite expensive, and often only printed on one side. If you want to use them, consider using those bordered papers for the cover, or as section dividers. (This could also save you the trouble of finding and scanning art.) Light-colored pages are going to provide the highest contrast with black ink, and are the easiest to read. Cream will have somewhat less glare than white. If you're not certain what color paper you want to use, see if you can purchase a single sheet of the colors you're considering (a print shop should be able to help you there), and print a single page out on the various colors and see what you like best. If you still can't decide, get a second opinion.

Printing

In addition to paying special attention to paper, the kind of printer you use is important. Ink-jet printers are nice and quick, but the ink is water soluble. Spill something wet on your cookbook pages, and it becomes a smeared and unreadable mess. You are definitely better off using a laser printer, or making copies on a photocopier from an original. You'll still have messy and stained pages, but at least the ink will still be legible.

Unless you have a photocopier in your home office, printing it yourself at home is really only suitable for a small number of cookbooks. The cost of replacing ink cartridges for desktop printers is quite high, and printing double-sided pages can be a hassle.

Binding

Have you decided how you're going to bind it? If you use report covers from the office supply stores, they're not expensive if you're only doing a few, around $5 for a pack of 5. Report covers are great for business presentations, but they're a bit drab for a cookbook. Use one with a clear front cover, so you can have your own artwork showing. Many will hold up to 100 sheets (that's a lot of recipes!), however, be aware that report covers won't allow your book to lay flat. That will hinder the use of the cookbook.

You could also use 3-ring binders, but please be aware that ink from the pages may stick to the plastic and peel off the paper, ruining your cookbook. The covers on those binders are bad for paper and archiving, unless it says somewhere on the label that it is *archival safe*. If it doesn't say anything, assume it is *not* archival quality. Archival binders are more expensive than regular binders, around $7 for a 1-inch capacity for archival quality, versus about $2 for one that's not. Avery makes an archival safe "EZD View Binder" that will hold a sheet on the cover (for your own artwork), and doesn't transfer print. It also has D rings, which hold more than typical round ring binders.

The disadvantages of binders: they are heavy, usually awkward, they don't fit on bookshelves, and are not particularly attractive. If you find them with clear pockets on the front, you can add your own front cover, and sometimes the spine, too. You do have the advantage of being able to add pages to the book, and they will lay flat. If you find affordable binders, you can use sheet protectors to keep your pages in. Sheet protectors run about $11 per package of 200 from an office supply store. (Check to see that they are archival safe!)

There is also the option of using binders that are used for scrapbooks or photo albums, which are archival quality, but they are even more expensive. They are also large and awkward and cumbersome in the kitchen, and, if they have cloth covers, stain-prone.

You can also purchase a machine you need to comb-bind at home, starting at about $65 for a "personal" model that will bind 90 sheets. You will also have the cost of the combs themselves ($7-12 for a box of 100 combs). Check your local office supply store for it, or look online. We were very lucky; my husband had comb-binding equipment at his office, and we just had to purchase the supplies. The disadvantage of comb-bindings is they can be pulled off the pages and can crack, but they're relatively inexpensive, and a comb-bound book will lay flat on a surface. That's a big plus for a reference book that you are constantly reading as you work!

Other binding options include Velobinding, spiral binding (plastic or metal coil), wire-o (similar to spiral) and saddle stitching (stapled in the centerfold). Of these five options, spiral binding with a plastic coil would be my first choice. The plastic coil doesn't crush and bend out of shape. Metal coil and wire-o bindings can crush and make a book difficult to use. Wire-o bindings can also be pulled out of shape, releasing the pages. Those three options will lay flat. Velobinding is a nifty binding method, involving plastic teeth, which get heated to a plastic strip along one side of the pages, melting the end of the teeth, preventing them from coming off. Nifty as it might be, books bound this way will not lay flat. To saddle stitch a booklet (this is only suitable for a small number of pages), you have to have a special kind of stapler that can reach into the crease where your centerfold is. Saddle stitching also messes up your pagination, since you will be using paper that has been folded in half, making each sheet of paper have four pages.

Printers

If you aren't going to do the printing and binding yourself, get pricing estimates from local and national chain printers. Calling is certainly going to be easiest, so sit down with your notebook and use the phone to get some estimates. If a few places sound promising, visit them, and see what kind of options they have; get price quotes in writing. Some will use your printed original, and others will accept your document on disk, there may be price differences between those two options, so be sure you ask about it.

Kinko's and CopyMax both offer online publishing options. You can upload a document, specify printing options from there, and get a cost estimate. With them, you have the option of picking your order up at the location you specify, or have it shipped to you.

Check your phone book for printers in your area. It's possible that you could get a better deal from someone locally than you could from a national chain. For fewer than 100 cookbooks, this may be your best option, since most of the publishing companies have minimum orders. There are two columns of printers in my local yellow pages. Some of those may not be able to accommodate book or booklet printing, but you won't know unless you ask. Get several estimates from different printers before you give anyone any money.

More than 100 copies, and you're probably better off using one of the cookbook publishers that cater to family reunion and fundraiser cookbooks. These companies have minimum orders as low as 100, but some have a minimum of 200. They have kits you can order to help you plan and publish your cookbook. You might also consider Athena Publishing, which has no minimum book order. I evaluate the kits and their pricing in the next chapter.

Additionally, there are a number of publishers online who will print your book. Some are "print on demand"—they will print your book one at a time, when someone orders a copy of it; others are "short-run" publishers—those who will print a small number of books at a time, all at once. The problem with print on demand (POD) or short-run publishing is that the author has to have money up front. With POD, the author has to pay a set-up fee, which can be quite high. With short-run, the smaller the number of books ordered, the higher the cost; the more you order, the lower the cost per book.

However, an advantage of using one of these types of publishers is that you have creative control. It's usually your cover art and your format, whereas with the fundraiser types of companies, you have to use their format and choose from their cover options. Some will allow you to design your own cover, for a fee.

Consider asking your family to contribute a little on the cost, unless you can afford to absorb it yourself. It will be helpful to gather those cost estimates before you contact family members to contribute financially, so that when you ask them to help with cost, you will know how much you need to ask for. $120 for 10 books might be a lot for one person to bear, but split 10 ways it's not so painful.

Please see **Publishers** *in the following chapter for these publishers' websites, contact information and addresses.*

TIP: Once you have your book printed and can admire the wonderful thing you have created, don't forget to archive your original! Save the computer file onto a CD if you have a CD burner at home, or ask a friend to do it if you don't. This will enable you to save it indefinitely, and also allow you to print out a copy later (perhaps as a graduation gift for a high school senior going off to college).

Organization

If you've done research about using a printer or a publisher for your cookbook, that information (price quote, minimum orders) should all be kept together in your accordion file, so it won't get misplaced.

If you are doing all the work yourself, and the family has agreed to share the costs with you, keep all of your receipts, so you can tell everyone what their share of the book was accurately. Have an envelope for those and put it in the accordion file.

Checklist

Have you:

1. Determined whether or not you are going to print your cookbook yourself?

2. Decided on the color and weight of the paper you will use?

3. Gotten price quotes from places who might do the copying for you?

4. Determined how you're going to bind it?

5. Gotten price quotes from places that might do the binding if you are not?

6. If you have more than 100 books to publish, can your family help you with the cost?

7. If so, have you determined what the cost per book is, so you know how much to ask people to contribute?

Chapter Eleven
Publishers

I contacted eight of the publishers listed below with general questions I wasn't able to get answered on their websites, like how many cookbooks they print a year, how many organizations/families they work with, and if they get repeat customers. Only three of them, Athena Publishing, Gateway Publishing and G&R Publishing, responded to my emailed questions. Since I didn't use any of these publishers personally, I cannot vouch for them. I evaluated their information packets from the standpoint of a potential customer, but also as a critic, comparing each business's offerings against the rest. Be sure you carefully read the information on their websites and any information they send you.

Prices go down with the volume of books ordered—the more you order, the lower the cost per book. Another thing that can drastically change the cost of your order is the number of recipes included. The more recipes you have, the thicker the book, and the more expensive it will be. That's something else to keep in mind when you collect your recipes.

With the cookbook publishers, I evaluated their packets and filled out their order forms, calculating how much a cookbook with 200 recipes, 10 "comments" and an index would cost, ordering 200 books. (My reasoning for that number is that some of the publishers have 200 books as their minimum, and to compare them all across the board, I needed identical orders from each.) With each of the publisher evaluations, I give you the cost I calculated per book, and what that bill would end up being, before freight and any applicable taxes.

Please note that email addresses and website URLs do change.

Athena Publishing, Inc.
4899 Hawkstone Road
Hilliard, OH 43026
Phone: 866-855-4899
Fax: 888-820-4849
webmaster@athenapublishing.net
http://www.athenapublishinginc.com/

Athena Publishing isn't exclusively cookbooks (they also do course packs for schools), but cookbooks is one of the things they promote on their website. This family-run business has an online recipe submission form, or you have the option of emailing them your cookbook as an attachment.

If you submit your recipes electronically, your cost per book for fewer than 50 books is $12-$26.50, depending on the number of recipes. It drops to $8-$16 for 50-99 books ordered. An order of 200 cookbooks, with 200 recipes, costs $7 per book for an order total of $1400. Where other companies charge for using custom artwork for covers and dividers, Athena offers that free of charge. Extra options include adding family tree information for $5 each page added to the order (not an extra $5 per book).

Athena has a 4- to 6-week turnaround from the time you submit your order to when you receive your books. That includes the week for checking and returning the proof copy they send the customer (free of charge). For customers who are doing their own layouts, the turnaround (and the cost) is less. They will keep a customer's information indefinitely in case reprints are requested.

According to Rachel Scofield, Athena's president, more and more people are requesting price quotes for just the printing process, having already done the layouts themselves. For those customers, Athena charges for the cost of printing and binding, and not labor. For people familiar with the desktop publishing process, this is a terrific break. However, Scofield says that there are all sorts of things that can, and do, go wrong with "camera-ready" copy. I would suggest calling or emailing them for what they suggest so as to avoid complications later.

The people I've contacted who have used Athena's publishing services have had nothing but praise for the company and the folks who run it.

*

Cafépress
Online, print on demand
http://www.cafepress.com/cp/info/sell/books.aspx

Cafépress was founded in 1999, starting with imprinting T-shirts with images their customers uploaded. They have greatly expanded their capabilities and can now custom-print just about anything, from tote bags and T-shirts to calendars and books.

With Cafépress, you download the size template you want to use and use it to make your book. You save the book in a PDF format and send it to them, and they print copies when there are orders for it. The advantage for you is that it costs you nothing to set up, and each person who wants a copy buys a copy from your "store," and you can set the price to be at cost, or raise it to make a profit. They currently only print in black and white, except for the cover, which is full-color.

In order to print with Cafépress, you have to set up a storefront. This is easy enough to do, all you need is an email address and a password. They'll also ask for your address, which they have to have so that you can receive royalty checks from items your storefront sells. If you raise the price above the base price, you will start to earn money on the things you have sold. While this may seem like a strange idea for printing a family cookbook, consider this: if you're having a family reunion, earnings from your cookbook could potentially pay for the reunion costs. It's also nice because you never have to buy a quantity ahead of time.

Just to see how simple the process was, I uploaded a modified version (no illustrations) of the cookbook I made for my family. The 93-page document, as an 8½-x-11-inch wire-o bound book costs $9.19. That's base price, no profit. It's really quite easy to do, and by raising the cost of the book to $10, that would earn me, the shopkeeper, 81¢ of profit for every book sold. Raise the cost to $12, and that profit increases to $2.81, and so on. Obviously, that's not going to raise a lot of money for your reunion, unless you sell a lot of cookbooks, or raise your profit to such a high number that no one wants to buy one, but it is an option. By including family T-shirts or other personalized items in the storefront you had to set up, you could raise additional funds.

*

Cookbook Publishers, Inc.
10800 Lakeview Avenue
P.O. Box 15920
Lenexa, KS 66285-5920
Phone: 800-227-7282 or 913-492-5900
Fax: 913-492-5947
info@cookbookpublishers.com
http://www.cookbookpublishers.com/

This family company has been in business since 1947. Their minimum book order is 100.

Their Publishing Kit

I received their kit 3 days after ordering it online. It arrived in a Priority Mail box, and contained no less than 13 items for my review, including a sample cookbook and a 52-page design selection book.

All in all, I am quite impressed with the materials they sent. It's all very slick and professional. After reading through the information, I get the feeling that they really know what they are doing, and that they care about me as a customer.

It took me about 15 minutes to fill out their 6-page order form, which is pretty easy to follow but has no line on which to figure the cost of your order. Just glancing at the order form does not reveal the cost, merely the cost of the options selected. Using the price chart and calculating any extras, reveals that my cost per book is $3.15

($3.05 base price, 10¢ per book for the extra comments I have provided). That makes my 200-book order $630. Half of that ($315) is due up front, with the order itself. The remaining balance plus freight charges is due before the books are shipped. (The payment schedule is different for organizations.) In none of the literature does it state any estimate for freight. "For your convenience, we pre-pay shipping costs. Then, we add the shipping costs to your invoice and provide you with additional free books which, when sold at our recommended prices, should generate enough money to pay for your freight expense." Personally, I would rather know what they were charging for freight.

Their turnaround on orders is 2 to 4 months, depending on the complexity and size of your order, and what time of year you place it. (July through December is their busy season.) They do not offer a proof option for customers to approve before the order is completed. Cookbook Publishers keeps your information for 2 years in case reprints are wanted or needed.

*

CopyMax
For online publishing options, go to http://www.copymax.com/.

How it works online: You make various selections in paper size and color, and how you want it bound. Once you've filled all that in, you'll get a price quote, and you can choose whether you want to pick it up at the store nearest you, or have it shipped. Then you upload the file you want them to print. My cookbook, at 96 pages of 8½-by-11-inch paper, a double-sided document with a clear cover and white glossy back cover, in black and white with a plastic comb binding, for 200 copies was quoted as being about $1194, before tax. Orders over $250 must be paid for up front. See your phone book for a location near you.

*

Fundcraft Publishing, Inc.
P. O. Box 340
410 Highway 72 W
Collierville, TN 38027
Phone: 901-853-7070
Fax: 901-853-6196
questions@fundcraft.com
http://www.fundcraft.com/

Fundcraft is the "original cookbook fundraising program," they claim. They have been making fundraiser and community cookbooks since 1942. They have expanded their offerings to include a print-on-demand option for books other than cookbooks (good to know if you're writing a family history). They have more than one program, with 100- and 200-book minimums, which makes them flexible to suit your individual needs.

Their Publishing Kit

The kit arrived 14 days after I ordered it from their website. The envelope contained 13 pieces of information, including their Get Cooking with Fundcraft CD, which I was pleased to see was available for both Windows® AND Macintosh® operating systems. A sample cookbook and a 31-page catalog of covers and dividers are also among the information sent.

As their name implies, Fundcraft is primarily geared towards selling fund raising cookbooks. The literature spends a lot of time on how much money can be made, and not so much on how to get the cookbook together in the first place. The guide is not terribly informative, and the supporting literature isn't, either.

It took me about 15 minutes to fill out their 6-page order form, which is straightforward but has no line on which to figure the cost of your order. Using the price chart shows that my cost per book is $3.10 for 200 recipes. That makes my 200-book order $620. To add "customer fillers" like recipe notes, it's an additional 25¢ per book, making the total $670. Fundcraft does not require money up front but allows 67 days to pay; half is due 37 days before the shipping date. The cost of freight is pre-paid, and they send extra books (3%

of the order, in my case, 6 free books) to sell to make up the freight charges.

Fundcraft has a turnaround of 4 weeks to 3 months depending on which program you choose. If you use their software and input the recipes yourself, it takes less time. A customer proof copy is available for a $25 fee. They keep the printing plates from your order for 5 years in case you need or want to reorder.

*

G&R Publishing
507 Industrial St.
Waverly, IA 50677
Phone: 800-383-1679
Fax: 800-886-7496
gandr@gandrpublishing.com
http://www.cookbookprinting.com/

Their website states they have "29 years and over 5 million books of experience." They also have a minimum book order of 100.

G&R prints from 275,000 to 300,000 books each year. (In November 2003, they had already passed 300,000.) Every year, they work with 400 to 500 individuals or organizations. 100 to 200 of those folks reorder books. Lory Trost, the woman who answered my questions, told me that it was difficult to put a number on how many of their customers are repeat customers. She said that sometimes a family will do a second volume, or someone from a church organization will come back to make a family cookbook (or vice versa).

She said that "a group or individual can take anywhere from a month to a year to put recipes together." Once G&R has the recipes and the order, they need about 8 to 10 weeks to complete it.

Their Publishing Kit

I received the kit 5 days after ordering online. The envelope included 4 pieces of literature. *Your Complete Guide to a Successful Custom Cookbook* is a 76-page guide that will help you get your committee organized, gathering the recipes, and choosing your options. There are 61 different cover options, or 16 different single-color covers. There are 3 different bindings to choose from, 5 different fonts and 4 cookbook formats, and various options at additional cost. A sample cookbook was also included.

Overall, I find the information from G&R to be helpful, clear and concise without bombarding me with too much. It is aimed primarily for fundraising cookbooks, and much of the information is geared for helping you get the most profit from your cookbooks. If you are using a cookbook to make money to fund a family reunion, you will find plenty of helpful advice to that end.

The 6-page order form took me 15 minutes to fill out. Theirs was the clearest of the long order forms to fill out. Unlike the other order forms, it has a price guide printed on the order form. Additionally, their order form *does* have a place to calculate an estimated price. My cost per book for 200 books with 200 recipes ended up being $3.75 plus 20¢ per book for notes, plus a charge of $25 for the indexing, making my order total $815. Families have to make a 50% deposit. Free books will be added to my order to cover the cost of shipping, which will be added to my invoice.

G&R processes and ships orders in about 3 months, including the time it takes to check the proof copy and send it back. The customer proof is free of charge. Information is kept for 5 years in case reorders are needed.

*

Gateway Publishing Company, Ltd.
US Office:
276 Cavalier Street
P.O. Box 559
Pembina, ND, 58271-0559
Phone: 800-665-4878

Canadian Office:
385 DeBaets Street
Winnipeg, MB R2J 4J8

Phone: 204.222.4294
Fax: 204.224.4410
Toll Free: 800-665-4878
cookbooks@gatebook.com
http://www.gatebook.com/

They've been publishing books since 1965. The minimum book order is 100 books. I spoke to Karen Velthuys about some of my questions. She didn't have an estimate for how many books they produce in a year but said they'd printed 12,000 in October (2003). They work with 400-500 organizations a year, and 20-30% of them end up placing an additional order for more books. Further, about 20-30% of their customers come back to do another cookbook with them. She also told me that from beginning to end (assuming all the recipes are gathered), publication takes about 5-6 weeks.

She asked me if I was looking to do a cookbook with them, and I explained that I was writing a book about making family cookbooks, since smaller families can't easily use the services of a cookbook publisher. Velthuys then commented that helping families with smaller print runs was something the company was looking into.

Their Publishing Kit

I received my kit from Gateway 10 days after ordering it. In the envelope were 7 items, including a form letter addressed to someone else (who probably got my letter)—an honest mistake. The letter urges me to call if I have any questions, and refer to the reference number on the letter, and on the very simple 2-page order form. There is a flyer about their new online cookbook system, with a 3-4-week turnaround (from the time you send them the online order. The final item is the "Let's Get Cooking" guide to putting your cookbook together. In it are some of the options you have to choose from. Not all of the options (like lamination) have the prices included on the order form; for that you have to call to get a quote.

This company may not list a hundred different options, but there is a very personal feel to the materials I received. Everything was clear and easy to understand.

The 2-page order form took less than 10 minutes to fill out and has a place to calculate the cost of the order. My price per book for 200 books (with 200 recipes) was $2.60, making my total $520. Half of that is due at the time of ordering, with the remaining balance (including freight) due on receipt of the books. To defray the cost of shipping, I would receive extra books equaling 3% of my order for free.

Gateway states their normal turnaround as 5 to 8 weeks, but that "projects done using our online system" take about half that time once submitted. They do not offer a customer proof option, suggesting instead to be a careful proofreader on your end and their proofreaders will do the same. Reorders placed within 90 days are discounted, and they hold on to the information for 2 years, unless a customer requests otherwise.

*

Kinko's
For online publishing options, go to http://www.kinkos.com/.

How it works online: First you upload your file, then you choose paper and binding options. Kinko's had fewer choices for options than were offered at the CopyMax website.

My cookbook, at 96 pages of 8½-by-11-inch paper, a double-sided document in black and white with a plastic comb binding, for 200 copies was quoted as being about $2230, before tax. See your phone book for a location near you.

*

Morris Press Cookbooks
3212 E. Hwy 30
Kearney, NE 68847
Phone: 800-445-6621
cookbooks@morriscookbooks.com
http://www.morriscookbooks.com

According to their website, they have been in this business since 1933. Their minimum book order is 200. I tried ordering their publishing kit online twice, and after 2 months of waiting, finally called for it. I received it in the mail about 2 weeks after the call.

Their Publishing Kit

The kit, when I received it, was huge. The box contained 10 items, including three different sample cookbooks: one softcover comb-bound, one hardcover comb-bound, and one three-ring binder. The large "publishing guide" contains 112 pages and many options for cover, dividers and recipe formats. There is a CD-ROM of their typensave™ software that you can use to type your own recipes and save money. Unfortunately, the software is only available for Windows®.

The 4-page order form took 10 minutes to complete. The order of 200 books with 200 recipes had a base price of $2.75 per book. With the addition of recipe notes, it's another 20¢ per book. The order comes to $550, with a discount of $60 if I use their software to enter the recipes myself, reducing my total to $490, or $2.45 per book

Using the information available on their website, I calculated that my 200-book order, with 270 recipes, would have a base price of $3.40 per book, making my order $680 plus freight. The cost of freight is defrayed by sending with the order an additional 3% free.

Morris's turnaround is 2 to 4 months, but they do have a computer submissions system (PCs only) that will cut that to about 2 months. Rush service is available but is not cheap: $250 or 20%, whichever is greater. They do offer a free customer proof, but "keeping proofs longer than 3 days will delay scheduled shipment." They hold on to your information for 5 years in case you need to reorder.

*

Rasmussen Company
US Office:
P.O. Box 268
152 West Rolette Street, # 7

Pembina, ND 58271
Phone: 800-665-0222
Fax: 204-694-6871
info@cookbookprinter.com
http://www.cookbookprinter.com

Canadian Office:
111 Plymouth Street
Winnipeg, MB R2X 2V5

Their minimum order is 200 books.

Their Publishing Kit

The Priority Mail envelope arrived 5 days after I ordered it online. It contained 7 different pieces of information for my review. It contained a 43-page guide and an example cookbook.

Rasmussen looks as though they would be the easiest of the listed publishers to deal with. There are not a huge number of choices, but that isn't necessarily a bad thing. After the dazzling variety offered by Cookbook Publishers Inc. and Morris Press, this simplicity is almost comforting.

Their 4-page order form took about ten minutes to fill out. It includes a place to calculate the cost of your order. My order of 200 books with 200 recipes and 10 comments calculated to $540: $2.70 per book plus 20¢ per book for the optional notes, for a total of $580. That includes the cost of shipping. Rasmussen includes shipping in the cost of their books, so there are no additional freight charges or free books to sell to cover those charges. This is nice to know; you know exactly how much your order will cost up front. It also means that they may be the least expensive of the cookbook publishers, since those other companies charge freight but don't include (or quote) its cost.

Rasmussen's estimated turnaround is about 2 months, with expected delays around Mother's Day and Christmas. A customer proof copy is available for $15. They keep your file for 3 years in case you need to reorder more copies.

*

Walter's Publishing
1050 8th St NE
Waseca, MN 56093
Phone: 800-447-3274
cookbook@hickorytech.net
http://www.custom-cookbooks.com/

Walter's has a number of different program options, including a family cookbook program (for which you can order a kit) that has as few as 25 books as the minimum order.

The information I ordered online came 18 days after I ordered it. Inside the slim envelope were a 19-page booklet, and 2 sheets of paper touting their Cookbooks Express and the Quick & Easy Family Cookbook organizer kit—which you have to order for $19.95 (that gets applied to your order of cookbooks; you're out the $20 if you don't print with them).

With a small order of 25 books, the price per book is rather high: $14.40-15.65. It drops dramatically the more books you order: $7.52-9.48 for a quantity of 50-74 books. My 200-recipe cookbook, at 200 copies, costs $2.75 per book, for a total cost of $550. It's costly to print only a few books, but when you only need a few cookbooks, there aren't many options.

Walter's expected turnaround time is about 9 weeks from submission for the family cookbook program. If they do the typesetting, customers will receive a proof copy. They hang on to your information for about 5 years in case you need to reorder.

Breakdown by Publisher

Except for Rasmussen, the quoted prices **do not** include shipping. Since their shipping is included, and the others' isn't, that probably makes them the least expensive option. Prices are for 200 books with 200 recipes, indexed, with 10 "comments/notes."

Gateway Publishing Co., Ltd.	$2.60/book, $520
Walter's Publishing	$2.75/book, $550
Morris Press Cookbooks	$2.75/book, $550
Fundcraft Publishers Inc.	$2.80/book, $560
Rasmussen Company*	$2.70/book, $40 notes, $580
Cookbook Publishers, Inc.	$3.05/book, $20 notes, $630
G&R Publishers	$3.75/book, $40 notes, $25 index, $815
Athena Publishing	$7.00/book, $1400

> TIP: Working with the larger publishers who specialize in cookbooks means you use their templates and their artwork unless you pay extra to use your own. With a smaller publisher like Athena, you have a great deal more creative control over the finished product.

Athena Publishing and Walter's Publishing are the only two from whom you can order fewer than 100 books.

To get estimates from CopyMax and Kinko's, I used their online order forms, and I used my own cookbook's page number to calculate the cost. For 200 comb-bound 8.5x11-inch, 48-page double-sided black-and-white books with a clear front cover and vinyl back, the estimates were (before tax):

CopyMax	$5.97/book, $1194
Kinko's	$11.15/book, $2230

CopyMax and Kinko's are clearly not the cheapest option, but you have complete creative control; all they do is the printing and binding. With the others, they are doing the typesetting and everything, but you have relatively little creative control.

Each of the publishers has their own merits. Visit the websites, order the kits, and that way you can determine which publisher will work better for *you*. Of all the publishers I contacted, I like dealing

---

* Cost includes shipping.

best with Athena; it's a very personal experience, and you can order in significantly smaller quantities.

Organization

Order the kits from the companies that sound best to you. I suggest you look at two to four different publishers to give you an idea of what they have to offer you. If you order all the kits, you may find yourself overwhelmed with information and choices. You need to know how many books you will need, since some of these publishers don't deal with quantities fewer than 200. You also need to have some idea of how many recipes you want to include. That will enable you to determine which publisher offers the best value for you.

Checklist

Have you:

1. Evaluated several companies and what they can offer?

2. Determined which options (index, photographs, etc.) you want?

3. Chosen a publisher?

4. Ordered more supplies from them (if necessary)?

Chapter Twelve
Alternatives to Print Publishing

If print-and-bind publishing seems cost-prohibitive, there are a number of different options to consider. Some of them are very time consuming and may not work within your time frame or don't lend themselves to making multiple copies. Other ideas may not be for everyone, or every family.

CD-ROM Cookbooks

If you have the ability to burn your own CDs, this might be a very convenient and inexpensive alternative to publishing. The best way to do this is to save your document as a PDF ("Portable Document Format"). Macintosh OS X has this capability built in, as do some PC programs: otherwise, you can buy Adobe Acrobat®, which is used to create PDFs. The advantage to using this format is that, with Acrobat Reader® (a free download), everyone who opens the document will see it exactly as you created it. When others will open your text document with their word processors, unless they have the same fonts loaded on their computers, the computer will change the font to something that is loaded on the machine (and probably mess up the pagination in the process, rendering your index useless). PDFs are seen exactly as they were saved and can be printed out if the person so desires.

Making a cookbook this way is great if everyone in your family has a computer. It's also a way of taking the cost of printing out of your hands, and letting the recipient print it out or not, as they choose. However, this obviously won't work for non-computer users. Another disadvantage is that Adobe Acrobat® is a $300 program. Before you buy it, make certain that software on your computer won't create these documents already.

Website Cookbooks

Another high-tech option to publishing is to put your recipes on a web page. There are many places that will help you build a website for free using their templates. If you are familiar and comfortable with HTML you can write your own pages with the help of a program like Microsoft FrontPage®, Adobe GoLive!® or Macromedia Dreamweaver®. If you already have a website, you can add the recipes to a section of that website. The recipes can be scanned images or they can be typed in as text. (Keep in mind that images on a web page slow down the load time.) If your family is far-flung and Internet savvy, this may be just the thing for you. People you have requested recipes from could even email you the recipes, typed out or as an image attachment. Now *that's* a 21st-century cookbook! Disadvantages of doing it this way include the cost of maintaining a personal website, the ads you deal with from free sites, and the inconvenience of having no computer in the kitchen. (If you have a computer in your kitchen, no problem there.) Additionally, free sites have limits to the amount of space your web page takes up, which does limit the amount you can put online. Text pages take up less space than image-rich pages, so there's one way to keep your storage totals down.

Photo Album Cookbooks

Take a photo album (your choice of size) that has sleeves for 4 x 6-inch photos. Make color copies of (or scan and print out) the recipes you want to include, crop them to the right size, and put them in the photo sleeves. That way, the recipients of your masterpiece will also have copies of the recipes in the handwriting of the person who submitted them. This works best if the recipes are already written on cards. The smaller 3½ x5-inch recipe cards can be enlarged slightly to make them fit better. Watch out for double-sided cards and make sure you get both sides copied!

If you want to avoid enlarging cards, simply give everyone 4x6-inch recipe cards and ask them to write their recipes on those cards, on one side only. You can purchase plain index cards, or special decorative recipe cards. Printing several copies of decorative recipe cards could be expensive (printer ink is not cheap, and color copies are substantially more expensive than black and white) or if you're making color copies of them. Also, those recipe cards usually have less writing space than a plain index card.

Another option to the index cards is to print the recipes out on cardstock that is perforated into 4x6-inch cards. Clipart can be used to decorate the cards, the same way you might use them in a document.

Photo albums come in a variety of sizes, from small pocket-sized ones that hold about a couple dozen photos/cards to the really large ones that have pages holding four photos to a page. I was lucky enough to find some with a food theme on the covers. You could choose one with a neutral cover and decorate it yourself with Con-Tact® paper or decoupage your own design.

There are some themes that lend themselves to this kind of cookbook. Showers and weddings make good applications for it, especially since you can leave room in the album for pictures taken at the event.

If you were to make a photo album cookbook, and have a copier make the photocopies for you, here's an idea of the cost: Say you make 10 albums, which hold 100 4x6-inch photos, and you paid $3 each for the albums. You can fit 3 4x6-inch cards on one 8½ x11-inch sheet of paper. That means you will make 33 pages, each with three recipes, for a total of 99 recipes. Photocopy each of those 33 pages 10 times, for 330 photocopies. That hundredth recipe could be written onto three cards, and then photocopied together on one sheet of paper 4 times, for a total of 12 copies of the same recipe (you'll have two extra). That calculates to 334 single-sided photocopied pages. For black and white copies, that will run around $27 (depending on the price of copies: I got a quote of 8¢/copy to calculate this.) For color copies, you can expect to pay around $231 dollars (69¢/copy). That makes the total cost $57 for black and white, or $261 for color. Your cost per book is about $5.70, or $26.10 for color. And this doesn't take into account the time spent to cut the cards apart.

Alternatively, you could give everyone 10 index (or recipe) cards and ask them to write the same recipe on each card. If their recipe needs more than one side of the card, ask them to use 2 cards. (This is not a good option if you have family members who are not comfortable writing due to arthritis or carpal tunnel syndrome.) White index cards are about $1 per pack of 100; "rainbow" packs are about twice that, and recipe cards can run around $30 per 100. Your cost with white index cards drops to about $34 dollars, or $3.40 per book.

Scrapbook Cookbooks

If you already have scrapbook supplies, you can also take that option, and create a scrapbook cookbook. I recommend this only if you're making one or two copies. It would get really exhausting and expensive to do more, but it's a perfect option as a wedding/anniversary/shower gift.

For a single book, you can make color copies of family recipes and print them on acid-free paper. Be sure you copy both sides of the recipe card, if needed, rather than having a two-sided copy. That way, you can mount the recipe on the scrapbook page however you choose, and not worry about whether it needs to come off the page to be used. I recommend that you use page protectors if you plan for the book to be used.

Scrapbooking pages come in many themes and colors, and there are thousands of stickers you can choose from to embellish further. There are kits available just for cookbook scrapbooks, and you're almost guaranteed to find just the right set of papers for you and your project.

If you do want to make more than one copy of your scrapbook cookbook, consider making a master copy, and then making more copies from that original. Once your pages are finished, scan them and save onto a CD, and either give out copies of the CD or print out the pages in color.

A scrapbook cookbook is a perfect gift. It's a loving collection, and a wonderful way to pass along those cherished recipes. *For more information and tips about scrapbooking, please see* **Resources** *in the Appendix*. For inspiration specifically about scrapbooking with recipes, read *Scrapbooking with Recipes*, by Susan M. Banker.

Recipe Notebook Cookbooks

If it isn't the publishing but the computing that makes you hesitate, consider a project that my grade school class once did. When I was in fourth grade, my teacher, Miss Shepard, had all of us bring in a recipe, written on a sheet of notebook paper. She mimeographed those pages, gave us all a copy of each other's recipes, and stapled our construction paper covers to them. It was a Christmas present for our moms and dads, and Mom has kept mine all these years. While the mimeograph has gone the way of the dinosaur, you can do the same thing and photocopy the sheets. You can also have the pages be double-sided. This would be a terrific advantage for longer recipes, since those rarely fit neatly on a card. You would also have a record of the person's handwriting. Just ask that people submit their recipes to you on a sheet of notebook paper—black ink would be best—and ask them to sign the bottom. (Or use the *Recipe Collection Form* in the Appendix if you want the recipes to be uniform in appearance.) Gather the recipes much the same way as you would on the computer, grouping then into sections, and get copies made. You can use some of the colorful specialty papers as section binders. (Paper Direct has the best selection of specialty papers I have seen; *see* **Resources** *for more information*.)

You can bind it with one of the options discussed the previous chapter, such as using binders or report covers. Or you can affix the copied pages onto scrapbook pages and embellish them as you see fit. If you use a binder, you might consider laminating the pages or using sheet protectors, for three reasons: it will keep the pages free of stains and protect them from wrinkles and tears, it will prevent the toner ink from lifting off the page, and it will also provide you with very clean pages to make copies from, should anyone request another copy of your cookbook.

Journal Cookbooks

You have probably seen the blank books like *I'm Writing My Own Cookbook*, designed for someone to jot down their favorite recipes. Those are not really conducive to making a family cookbook, and they just seem commercial and impersonal.

However, you could take a variation on that theme, and take a blank book, such as the ones used for journals, and carefully write recipes down in it. That's a great idea for a single person, with a single collection, right? So how would it work as a family cookbook?

If you intend to give the book as a gift, first ask your contributors if they would be willing to handwrite their contributions in the book. Then pass the book from person to person until you've collected all the recipes you set out to get. If the contributors are spread all over the country, this could be a long and drawn-out project as the book moves from person to person. But it could be done! And even though the postal service is far from perfect, it's kind of a neat idea to think of a cookbook traveling all over the country (perhaps the world!), getting more and more full as it travels from place to place. If your family is a bit more locally concentrated, you could take the book to the people who were contributing and then take it to the next person when they were finished. This would be a wonderful handwritten heirloom.

Another way to get more than one copy of this cookbook would be to buy a few copies of the blank books and give all of them to the first person on the list, explaining that you need a copy of the recipe(s) to go into each of the blank books. Then it would work the same way as above, except you would end up with more than one filled book when everyone has contributed. A word of caution: This won't work for many copies. More than five risks writer's cramp and illegible recipes in the last book in the stack, and physical limitations of the contributors may also be a factor.

Another disadvantage to using blank books is that unless you purchase spiral- or comb-bound books, they will not lie flat and be difficult to use for cooking. Additionally, if the cover is cloth, it's not really appropriate for the kitchen.

If this sounds like your idea of the perfect record for those family recipes, check your local bookstore for blank books. If you can't find what you're looking for there, try a stationery store, or go online to Amazon.com.

Hand-Tied Recipe Booklets

If you only plan to make a few cookbooks, and only plan on a limited number of recipes, you can make your own booklets, tied together with yarn or ribbon. Simply use a hole punch on the crease near the top and bottom (you will want to measure and mark where you put the holes, so they all line up), and weave ribbon or yarn through the holes.

If you use your computer, set your pages up in "landscape" format (horizontal). Make two columns and enter your recipes, leaving about 2 inches of room in the center margin. Since it's such a short booklet, page numbers and an index aren't really needed. These can be a little tricky: print the samples to make sure you've got the columns centered just right while leaving room in the centerfold for the holes.

If you don't want to fold the pages in half, they can also be cut. An 8½- x-11-inch piece of paper can be cut into four pieces of 4¼ x 5½ inches and tied together. A 12-inch square sheet of scrapbook paper can be cut into four pieces that are 6 inches square. There are lots of ways to make a smaller book out of larger sheets of paper, and many ways to tie/sew them together. Check out a book about bookbinding techniques if that's your interest. *See* **Bibliography**.

Given the low number of pages in a booklet, these could also be handwritten, assuming your handwriting is legible (mine isn't). One trick I have used to write in a straight line on unlined paper is to put a sheet of notebook paper behind what I'm writing on. That only works on relatively lightweight paper (20 lb.), however. If you use layout paper, it has a pale grid for keeping your lines straight which doesn't photocopy, and it will help you keep your lines and margins neat.

I made a Christmas-themed booklet as a gift for my daughter's teacher, using cardstock for the cover and 4 interior sheets. Folded in half, that makes 16 pages, on which I fit 17 recipes and lyrics from Christmas carols at the bottoms of some of the pages.

The cost, for 5 printed pages, is going to be around $2 per book (for black and white) if you have the pages photocopied. A 10-yard spool of 1/8-inch ribbon will do at least 10 booklets, and costs about $1.

Another way to make hand-tied booklets is to punch small holes and sew the pages together with heavyweight thread, yarn or hemp. Specialty paper retailers sell pre-printed postcards that come 4 to an 8½-x-11-inch sheet. Those can be run through an ink-jet or laser printer to make colorful and thematic covers for your booklet. Also, by using a 4¼-x-5½-inch format, you get 4 pages per standard sheet of bond paper. That will limit you to a single recipe per page, unless they're *really* short, and it can be tricky to make sure your margins are clear so that you can print on both sides without clipping off part of the recipes when you cut apart the sheets. But if you used a template (which many of the specialty paper retailers sell for their products), it could be done quickly and easily. Now all you need is a paper cutter!

> IDEA: Booklets make wonderful party favors, too! The theme of your party could be reflected in the theme of your cookbook.

Organization

If you are not going to use a publishing/binding method for your cookbook, you will need to gather the supplies for how you are going to put it together. Photo albums or scrapbooks will need to be purchased, as well as index cards or special paper. Keep everything together until you're ready to start, so you don't have to hunt for things when you are.

Checklist

Have you:

1. Decided not to print-and-bind your cookbook?

2. Chosen an alternative?

3. Determined the supplies you need?

4. Gathered all your materials together?

Chapter Thirteen
Archiving

Many people don't have any idea of where to begin archiving, or how to archive. For me, the archival process begins with using my computer to scan photographs and recipes. The recipes can then be printed out on acid-free paper in color to preserve the look and feel of the original. The scanned images should be burned onto a CD and can be kept a long time if handled with care. CDs themselves do have a fixed lifespan—you can buy archival-grade CDs, which usually include storage instructions to maximize life.

Originals should be stored in a cool, dry place. Don't store photos or other papers in airtight containers, though this may be your first inclination. Doing so traps any present moisture in with the documents, which could ruin them. Keep them out of sunlight; ultraviolet light is not good for photos or papers.

Don't store news clippings next to photos, and don't store negatives with photos, for two reasons: newspaper is acidic—very bad for photos, and if something catastrophic happens, you've lost the photo AND the negative. Additionally, negatives contain chemicals, which can degrade pictures.

There is a product called *Archival Mist®*, that is rather expensive. It's a neutralizing substance you spray on paper, rendering it acid-free. A 1.5-oz. can of the stuff is going to run around $16. The company claims that it extends the life of the paper five times (10 years to 50, for instance), and that a single application protects the document for the lifetime of that document. It can be purchased from most places that sell scrapbook supplies.

If you borrow recipes either to scan or to hand-copy, you should also make a record of what you're borrowing, its physical description as well as a description of the contents. You are essentially researching, and you should cite your sources. On the CDs that contain the scans of my Grandma Boughner's recipes, there are two documents, Index and Notes. Index contains a list of all the recipes and the name of the image, *i.e.*: "14.jpg—Chocolate Cookie Sheet Cake (handwritten, 'Rosie')." With every image, I give the name of the recipe (or recipes), and indicate the format of the recipe, whether it is handwritten, a newspaper clipping, or from packaging. Here are my notes for that recipe box:

These are the scanned recipes from the recipe box that belonged to **Mabel Thompson Boughner, last residing in Hattiesburg, MS** (1). The box is currently in the possession of her elder daughter, **Janice Boughner Hoggard, currently of Hattiesburg** (2). Janice kindly lent the box to me so that I could scan the recipes that were inside.

There are **ninety-one scanned images** (3) of recipes. They are **written on cards, taken from packaging, written on handy slips of paper** (4). Some are in **hardly-used condition** (5), while others are stained with wear and age. Some of the recipes have **names and dates** (6), including contributions from "Lois H." and "Rosie." A couple of recipes give clues as to who gave Mabel that particular recipe: Lime Pickles are from "Hazel"—likely Mabel's mother-in-law, Hazel Martin Boughner Reed; "Aunt Callie Fruitcake" is Callie Cannon Dickinson, Mabel's mother's sister. Some of the recipes are recognized to be in Mabel's youngest child, Debbie Boughner Stewart's, youthful handwriting.

Each scan is as true to the original as possible and still remain readable. Some of the originals were hard to read from stains; where needed, **words were traced** (7) so that the scanned image, if reproduced, would yield a readable text. (Nothing can be done about the quality of the handwriting, however.) Images were scanned over a two-day period: **August 7–8, 2001** (8). The **picture of the face of the recipe box** (9) is not Mabel's box, but it is the same style. It was purchased to have a copy of the same Stylecraft box Mabel used, just as the recipes are all copies.

It is my intention to transcribe the recipes, in addition to having the scanned images, so that there is a text file (producing a hard copy) and the image file. The transcription will be indexed, as well.

Wendy Boughner Whipple (10)
Tuesday, March 5, 2002 (11)
Matteson, IL (12)

1. Who the recipes belong(ed) to, and where they last lived.
2. Who currently has the recipes, and where they now live.
3. How many scanned images there are.
4. What the recipes are; cards, clippings, packaging.
5. The condition of the recipes.
6. Mention of the non-recipe contents.
7. Mention of any digital restoration.
8. When the recipes were scanned.
9. Comment regarding the box itself.
10. Who scanned them.
11. When was the note written.
12. Where was the note written.

What I didn't say in the notes that I should have is that Rosie and Lois H. are friends of Mabel's from Danville, Illinois. Because I was in a hurry to return the recipe box to my aunt, I forgot to photograph the box, and I purchased a box just like it. I also don't describe the box itself, or its condition, which I should have done.

> HINT: Don't get in such a hurry that you forget important information!

Doubtless, some people will believe that this was overkill, that I went to far more trouble than was necessary for a few recipes. But in addition to being an avid recipe collector, I am also the family historian. Preserving the information in the way I did enables generations behind me to read my notes and know exactly where those recipes came from, and even what the box that Grandma kept them in looked like.

For instance, say you borrow a recipe box with 160 pieces inside. Working steadily with your computer, you can expect to take about 7 hours scanning them, with some family interruptions. That is with putting the recipes on the scanner bed, scanning and saving each recipe as a separate image (making sure to get both sides of a card as one larger image). This is methodical, tedious work. The way I start is to create a new folder on my computer, and save the images into that folder. When I am finished scanning, I can then burn the whole folder full of images onto a CD. Depending on the condition of the recipes, I may or may not alter the color/contrast. If the recipes are readable as-is, I don't usually bother to brighten them unless I plan to print them out. That process takes even longer than the scanning!

I scan at 300dpi (dots per inch), which enables me to enlarge the images and make digital repairs. Those repairs might consist of filling in part of a clipped-off word or adjusting the color and contrast of badly yellowed items. Scanned at that resolution, the image will print very well. I do not recommend scanning below 96dpi, or your text won't be as crisp. If you're scanning them to put online, 72dpi is fine (and will let your pages load faster), but that's not a good resolution for printing.

While you have a choice of many different formats to save your digital artwork, TIFF might be a better option than JPEG. JPEGs are "lossy"—they tend to lose data when they are compressed and reopened, eventually degrading the quality of your image. TIFFs are "loss-less," can be set to "no compression," which means no data lost.

I also recommend that when you make an archive CD, you make more than one copy. Always offer a CD to the owner of the information you're scanning; it's only polite. If you make additional copies to share, that also helps to preserve the information in more than one location, in case something should happen to the copy in your possession.

CDs won't last forever, but if properly cared for, they will last a long time, potentially decades. Try to keep your discs in a cool, dry place, away from sunlight (which will heat up the disc). Some people also suggest that storing them vertically in their cases will prolong the life of a CD, as they can warp if stored horizontally. As noted earlier, you can also buy archival-quality CDs.

If there are changes in format, like a new version of MS Word®, periodically update any document files on the CD and write them to a new CD. TIFF, GIF and JPEG are standard formats now, but be sure to follow trends in data, and update old file formats, which may become obsolete, and impossible to open with new software that no longer uses that format.

There are two books by authors I highly recommend: *Organizing and Preserving Your Heirloom Documents* by Katherine Scott Sturdevant, and *Preserving Your Family Photographs* by Maureen A. Taylor. Sturdevant's book has lots of very helpful advice on preserving documents. Taylor, too, offers valuable information on taking care of those old photos. The advice in those books will greatly help the novice archivist, and likely more experienced ones as well.

There are also a number of websites that deal with archiving and restoration. I am not an expert on this, and I hope that if you really want to preserve your family's documents and photographs, you will seek professional advice. The Library of Congress has an FAQ (frequently asked questions) page on this topic: http://lcweb.loc.gov/ preserv/presfaq.html, dealing with documents, photos and books.

One more suggestion about archiving: After you've distributed the copies you've made to family members, consider contributing a copy to your local public library or genealogical society. The addition of all that family trivia and history will make your cookbook a valuable research tool for genealogists in the future. If you do decide to do this, make sure that all of your family members are also okay with the idea.

Organization

After you've scanned those recipes, don't forget to type up your notes about the box (or file, or notebook): who owned it previously (if applicable), where and when they lived last, who owns it now, how many pieces it contains and their condition, who scanned the contents and when. Describe the condition of the box that holds them as well, with as much detail as you can. Check the bottom of the box or inside to see who manufactured it, record that information, and describe how it's decorated (if it is). Save all of this information onto a CD, and keep that in a cool, dark place. If you make more than one copy of the CD, you can distribute it to other family members; that shares the treasure and helps to preserve the information in more than one location.

Checklist

Have you:

1. Gathered the materials you intend to archive?

2. Carefully scanned the recipes?

3. Typed up notes about where those recipes came from?

4. Saved the recipes and your notes onto a CD?

5. Carefully stored all the materials so as to maximize their storage lifespans?

Chapter Fourteen
About Copyrights

Copyrights are the rights of an individual author or artist to the works they have created. Copyrights are created when the work is created, whether or not the copyright is registered with the US Copyrights Office in Washington, DC (for American works). These rights protect the owner of the intellectual property from the exploitation of their works. *For more information about this, see* http://www.copyright.gov.

It is important to know that if you are using recipes from a cookbook (ones that have been used by a relative for years), the way in which the recipe is written is copyrighted by the author. To avoid this infringement, the instructions must be rewritten in your own words. The ingredients themselves are not copyrightable, as they are a method, and methods cannot be copyrighted. Some names of recipes (like Derby Pie) *are* copyrighted, or trademarked, and cannot be used. If your recipe's ingredients call for a specific brand of something (like Snicker® Pie), you may use the name of the brand without any problems. However, if your recipe does not require a specific brand, (like Jell-O®), "gelatin" should be used instead.

When using clipart, you need to know if it is royalty-free or not. Some places online allow you to use their art, so long as you are not using it for commercial purposes. When in doubt, contact the artist and ask for their permission to use their art, and tell them your intended use. If you are not planning on selling your cookbook (like in a fundraiser), you should have no problems obtaining permission.

Things that are public domain or royalty-free may be used without the concern of whether you are infringing on another's copyright. Although the Internet is a marvelous source for graphics, unless it says somewhere on the page that the graphics are free to use by anyone who wants it, assume that the art is copyrighted and do not use it without contacting the artist and gaining their permission.

"Fair use" is a term that refers to the ability of an individual to use parts of a copyrighted work without infringement. Fair use is for when parts of a work are quoted for reviews, research, or educational purposes. It is *not* fair use to co-opt entire portions of a copyrighted work to add to your own work, as with adding a recipe in its entirety. It takes just a little effort to rewrite a recipe in your own words, or to obtain permission from an artist before using their art.

Don't think that because your family cookbook is not going to be sold, because it's only for family, or because it's only a few copies, it doesn't count. It *does* count. Artists and authors work very hard for the things they produce. Using their work without permission is theft, and it's not right. Please keep this in mind when you are making your cookbooks, and honor the rights of those other artists and authors. Remember, once you put your cookbook together, *you* are now a copyright holder.

Resources

Genealogy

Cyndi's List: The Cyndi of this website is Cyndi Howells, author and speaker. Her site is a massive collection of genealogical links. http://www.cyndislist.com

Family Search: This is the website for the Latter Day Saints (Mormons). Among other things at this site is the entire 1880 US census in a searchable database. http://www.familysearch.org

US GenWeb: This is a database of state and county genealogy websites. Some of the sites have a great deal of very helpful information. http://www.usgenweb.com

Ancestry and **RootsWeb**: Ancestry is a partially free, partially subscription-based website with a great deal of information. Ancestry "supports" RootsWeb, which is all free information. Both have search engines on the sites to look for your ancestors. RootsWeb has a number of message boards and e-mailing lists. http://www.ancestry.com and http://www.rootsweb.com

LeisterPro: Maker of Reunion® for Macintosh computers, it is a terrific genealogy program for the Mac user. http://www.leisterpro.com

Family Tree Maker®: A Windows-only genealogy program. (They used to make a Mac version; they no longer do.) http://www.genealogy.com

Archiving

Library of Congress: Information and advice for preserving and archiving your collections. http://www.loc.gov/preserv/

Northeast Document Conservation Center: Their website has lots of good information for how to preserve and care for your documents, photos and books. http://www.nedcc.org

Archival Suppliers: This site has a large selection of archiving products, from deacidification sprays to environmental monitoring equipment. Order a catalog from their website. http://www.archivalsuppliers.com

Clipart & Fonts

There are many sources online for clipart. A search in your favorite search engine for "clipart" will give you more sites than you can believe. It's much the same with fonts, but here are a couple of my favorite sources:

Font Magic: This site is well-organized, and has fonts grouped by category. For Windows®. http://www.fontmagic.com

Blue Vinyl Fonts: Some free and some available for purchase, both Macs® and Windows®, and really unique! http://www.bvfonts.com

Dover Publications: Black-and-white clipart series with many themes and styles to choose from. Clipart is also available on CD-ROMs. Catalogs are available to order from the website. http://www.doverpublications.com

Specialty Paper

Paper Direct
PaperDirect Internet
1025 East Woodmen Road
Colorado Springs, CO 80920

Phone: 800-272-7377
International orders (outside 48 contiguous US states, Canada, or US territories) call: 800-865-8634
Fax: 800-443-2973
customerservice@paperdirect.com
http://www.paperdirect.com/

Call or go online to order their free catalog, or order directly from the website. Their 8½-x-11-inch PaperFrames™ come in more than 350 styles and are ideal for section dividers. Some even have food-related themes, and there are many occasion themes, as well. The 28-lb. sheets come in packages of 100.

4PapersPlus.com
738 Madison Street, Brooklyn NY 11221
Phone: 718-452-4400
Fax: 718-452-4545
http://www.4paperplus.com

Their online catalog features themed pre-printed papers with more than 40 designs in the Food/Menu category, as well as special occasion and seasonal themes. The 8½-x-11-inch sheets come in packages of 25 (24-lb). bond paper.

DECAdry PC Papers
http://www.decadry.com

The online catalog is available in English, French, German, Dutch, Italian and Spanish. They are an international company with a nice selection of 8½-x-11-inch pre-printed papers that come in packs of 100, 50 or 25. They do not currently sell in the United States or Canada, but Europe, South America and Asia have dealers. If you live outside North America, this would be an excellent source of papers for you.

Scrapbooking Sources

Creative Scrapbooking
http://www.creativescrapbooking.com
Publishers of *Creating Keepsakes Magazine* and *Memory Makers Magazine*, their website also lists scrapbook supply stores by state.

Scrapbooking.com
http://www.scrapbooking.com
An online scrapbooking magazine.

Scrapbook Storytelling
The book *Scrapbook Storytelling*, by Joanna Campbell Slan (©1999), has a lot of lovely and lively examples to inspire you. She also has a website: http://www.scrapbookstorytelling.com.

Bibliography

Adams, Marcia. *Recipes Remembered*. Gramercy Books: New York, NY. 1995.

Allen, Mary Emma. "Writing Your Family Food Heritage." *Old Fashioned Living*. 1999. http://www.oldfashionedliving.com/heritage.html (4 Nov 2003).

Banker, Susan M. *Scrapbooking with Recipes*. Meredith Publishing Group: Des Moines, IA. 2003.

Beach, Mark and Eric Kenly. *Getting it Printed, third edition*. North Light Books: Cincinnati, OH. 1999.

Devall, Sandra Lentz. *Desktop Publishing Style Guide*. Delmar Publishers: Albany, NY. 1998.

Golden, Alisa. *Creating Handmade Books*. Sterling Publishing Company: New York. 1998.

Goulart, Frances Sheridan. *How to Write a Cookbook—And Sell It*. Ashley Books: Port Washington, NY. 1980.

Hays, Rolfs & Associates. *How to Write and Publish a Classic Cookbook*. New American Library: New York. 1986.

Hickman, Alyssa. "A Recipe for Family History." *Family Education Network*.

http://www.familyeducation.com/article/0,1120,22-12207,00.html (4 Nov 2003).

Kenzle, Linda Fry. *Pages: Innovative Bookmaking Techniques.* Krause Publications: Iola, WI. 1997.

Kleback, Linda. "Recipes Can Be Full of Family Memories." *D'Addezio.com.* Originally published in the Sunday, January 25, 1998 edition of *The News Herald*, Panama City, FL. http://www.daddezio.com/genealogy/articles/recipe.html (4 Nov 2003).

LaPlantz, Shereen. *Cover to Cover: Creative Techniques for Making Beautiful Books, Journals & Albums.* Lark Books: Asheville, NC. 1995.

Mohler, Mary. "Timeless Traditions." *Parents Magazine.* December 2003. Harlan, IA.

Parker, Roger C. *Looking Good In Print, third edition.* Ventana Press: Research Triangle Park, NC. 1993.

------. *Looking Good in Print, fifth edition.* Paraglyph Press: Scottsdale, AZ. 2003.

Pitzer, Sara. *How to Write a Cookbook and Get It Published.* Writer's Digest Books: Cincinnati, OH. 1984.

Poynter, Dan. *Publishing Short-Run Books, fourth edition.* Para Publishing: Santa Barbara, CA. 1987.

Rehmel, Judy. *So, You Want to Write a Cookbook!.* Marathon International Publishing Company: Louisville, KY. 1984

Richards, Constance E. *Making Books and Journals: 20 Great Weekend Projects.* Lark Books: Asheville, NC. 1999.

Richardson, Lou and Genevieve Callahan. *How to Write for Homemakers.* Iowa State College Press: Ames, IA. 1949.

Schmidt, R. Marilyn. *How to Write and Publish a Family Cookbook.* Pine Barrens Press: Barnegat Light, NJ. 1995.

Slan. Joanna Campbell. *Scrapbook Storytelling.* EFG, Inc.: Cincinnati, OH. 1999.

Steligo, Kathy. *Meals and Memories: How to Create Keepsake Cookbooks.* Carlo Press: San Carlos, CA. 1999.

Stewart, Martha. "A Gift for Mom to Cherish." *The Holland Sentinel Online.* 1 May 2000. http://www.thehollandsentinel.net/stories/ 050100/fea_mstewart.html (4 Nov 2003).

Sturdevant, Katherine Scott. *Bringing Your Family History to Life Through Social History.* Betterway Books: Cincinnati, OH. 2000.

------. *Organizing & Preserving Your Heirloom Documents.* Betterway Books: Cincinnati, OH. 2002.

Taylor, Maureen A. *Preserving Your Family Photographs.* Betterway Books: Cincinnati, OH. 2001.

Townsend, Doris McFerran. *The Way to Write and Publish a Cookbook.* St. Martin's Press: New York. 1985.

Wolfe, Kevin J. *You Can Write a Cookbook.* Writer's Digest Books: Cincinnati, OH. 2000.

Index

If you have any questions, comments, success (or not so successful) stories you'd like to share, please contact me. I'd love to hear from you! If your ideas are used in a future edition of this book, you will receive a free gift!

Wendy A. B. Whipple
954 Dartmouth Ave.
Matteson, IL 60443-1515

http://www.CreatingAnHeirloom.com
wendy@creatinganheirloom.com.

The website includes even more useful links and information and is updated often. Thank you!

—

Autism is a rising epidemic among our children. Chances are you know someone with autism, or know someone else who does. Please read The Autism Experience: Stories of Hope and Love, *edited by Karen Simmons and Murray Hoke, available at http://www.autismtoday.com. The author contributed an essay to* The Autism Experience, *entitled "We'll Do What We Have to Do," relating her family's experience after their daughter was diagnosed with autism, in December of 2000.*

LaVergne, TN USA
28 December 2009
168180LV00005B/4/A